1

Jackpot Nation

Jackpot Nation

*Rambling and Gambling
Across Our Landscape of Luck*

Richard Hoffer

HarperCollins*Publishers*

FIRST EDITION

Designed by Joseph Rutt

Library of Congress Cataloging-in-Publication Data is available upon request.

ISBN: 978-0-06-076144-8
ISBN-10: 0-06-076144-X

07 08 09 10 11   NMSG/RRD   10 9 8 7 6 5 4 3 2 1

To Carol

Jackpot Nation

Introduction

It takes no great social historian to explain the American tendency toward risk-reward schemes, both dubious and legitimate. This country, as far as that goes, was founded on a flier. And every possible advancement in knowledge and wealth has been occasioned by some fantastic bet. We were always, just by virtue of our pioneer origins, in the game of speculation. Gold Rush, anybody? Or just a hundred shares of Pet.com? By now, through a couple hundred years of just this kind of political and economic evolution, we have been so thoroughly self-selected for risk-taking that only a righteous few of us can avoid scanning life's tote board first thing in the morning.

Good thing, when it comes to settling a nation or jetting off to the moon. Or even starting up Yahoo! Or asking that girl, too smart and too pretty for the likes of us, to marry us. Hard to imagine where this country would be if our ambition were restricted to sure shots, if we weren't careless enough in our greed to ignore long odds. I guess we'd still be in England and nobody would have iPods. Also, there would be a lot of bachelors. But what happens when this native predisposition toward risk-taking—now encouraged by civic institutions, a travel industry, a technology boom, a yawning void of recreation, a collapse in that old-time religion—becomes so pervasive that nearly every aspect of our culture is now a function of chance?

Well, I was curious. So, with little more than my own personal treasure map (I can see where more judgmental minds might call it Satan's TripTik—but not me) and cash advance access on four credit cards, I embarked on my own little road to ruin, exploring our landscape of luck. I didn't set out to participate—although there I was, spinning for sausages in St. Paul and waiting for the river in Salt Lake City (and yes, I did max out those cards, but that's another story) and standing in the Caesars Palace sports book holding a paper sack filled with $100,000 (and that's really another story)—but to investigate, to discover where and how we flex that muscle, which you might have thought vestigial by now, certainly flabby. Turns out there's a humming and thrumming economy out there, never mind our government, totally invested in its exercise.

You think this is Fast Food Nation? We Americans bet each other about $80 billion last year, more than we spent on movie tickets, CDs, theme parks, spectator sports, and video games—combined! It's more than we spent on higher education (and only a little bit less than we spent on fast food, which has the advantage of a drive-thru; the day you can take Phoenix and give six at a curbside clown, that advantage will certainly be eliminated). And, due to a confluence of trends that make it easier and ever more acceptable to gamble, we will increase that action year by year until the daily double really is more important to our economy than a double-double already is. It is impossible to know what limits there might be to such growth when our lottery libido is unleashed by civic and moral approval, not to mention Internet access. Whatever taboos there might have once been (our riverboat mentality was, for most of our history, held somewhat in check by the reigning values of hard work and self-sacrifice and Protestant morality) have fallen at such a pace that a backroom activity has become a parlor game.

But why wouldn't this country be devoted to the pursuit of luck? Like I say, the timid were left behind when the *May-*

flower sailed, the resulting start-up population already inclined toward overconfidence, a belief in destiny. But, really, what did we ever find here to discourage our sense of entitlement? Ever since we arrived, and once we relieved the Indians of their management (again, another story), it's been one windfall after another. No wonder good luck has come to seem our rightful condition. The abundance, however accidental (kind of a definition of luck), has been simply stupefying.

It's been Jackpot Nation from day one, as we've stumbled from gold strike to gusher. American history is a timeline of providence, an epoch of flabbergasting discovery. Mother lodes, wide-open prairies, vast buffalo herds, timberland: Who among our adventuring forebears ever set out to chart this wilderness and was disappointed? Who took a chance and crapped out?

This is surely our rightful condition. The idea of a payoff, whereby some small amount of industry gets applied to any crazy notion and returns investments in wild multiples, has come to seem a constitutional right. The original groundwork for such national confidence was purely a product of our natural resources. But as these were explored and exhausted, our native wit became an equally valuable source of capital. We were as good at developing things as at stumbling upon them. Maybe it was the miracle of (mostly) economic democracy, but smarts became highly incentivized. In this country anyway, it was ridiculously easy to parlay ideas into wealth and power. Maybe nobody's come up with a better mousetrap, but there's been no end to the refinement of gadgetry to enrich our lives—or at least its inventor.

It's been a get-rich-quick country from day one, everybody's life animated by the certainty of opportunity. We very well could discover gold, but failing that (say we prefer indoor work), we might improve our lot marketing vitamins or dabbling in foreclosures. Basically, it's there for the taking.

It's been the work of religion (and, once upon a time, our government) to deny, or at least counter the element of luck, which, after all, would dampen the instinct toward holy striving. Something for nothing never squared with our Puritan origins, even though the team logo back then was a cornucopia. But to deny this continued good fortune, to ignore American serendipity, is another kind of arrogance, too. Do we really deserve what we get? Have we really earned all that we have?

Surely there is another part of us that understands, as smart as we are and as hard as we work, we've cashed a ticket just by being American. And if you don't appreciate that fact, take your Subway franchise to Darfur. Let me know how your expansion plans work out.

To be an American is to be emboldened by our long run of luck, to be ready for every opportunity, to ante up as soon as the cards are shuffled. This has made for a pretty exciting nation, with a lot of entertaining foolishness, of course. We've also enjoyed a lot more progress than less adventuresome countries. Hands up, who else has the right to vote *and* has video-on-demand?

But to be an American these days, now that all the really good adventures have been achieved, has meant a gradual retreat into the safety of choice. It's no longer necessary to load the kids into a covered wagon and head West, fighting Indians along the way, to get ahead. Far easier just to take on a little overtime, or buy rental properties. Still, that appetite for risk remains and it's up to us to satisfy it within the confines of our twenty-first-century comfort. Granted, we no longer face the somewhat daunting prospect of being scalped, but we still need the make-believe of mastery, which is why we have paintball, infomercial get-rich schemes, and all these other arenas of simulated survival.

We've always (seems like always) had Las Vegas, too. It's been our testing grounds for the detonation of statistical TNT (and family values, and architectural insanity) for a hundred years now. It's been the frontier where we work out our inclination toward risk-taking, but with clean sheets and magic shows. And it's also been part of that double standard by which our gambling roots can both be embraced and denied. It's securely quarantined in the Nevada desert; its very remoteness has guaranteed its success. Sin City, maybe, but at least it's required the effort of travel. Put it this way: Anybody smart enough to book a holiday package to Las Vegas will not be shocked by the concept of recreational overhead. The $199 barrier of entry that the Stratosphere might require may be slight, but at least it weeds out the merrymakers who might otherwise put the college fund on black. Neither church groups nor band camps ever wander into Las Vegas by accident.

Thing is, that's all changed. There is now—quite suddenly, it seems—the kind of encouragement from our government and legitimate industry that requires us to gamble, and to be able to do it wherever is most convenient for us. Casinos are no longer in legal isolation, but everywhere. With the redress of the American Indians, which gave them casino rights in every state but Hawaii and the reliably uptight Utah, there is hardly anybody more than twenty minutes from a slot machine (I live in Santa Barbara, California, a remote seaside resort; I am twenty minutes from a slot machine). What was once a contained contamination has now spread coast-to-coast, and it no longer has any viral connotations.

And that's not even the half of it. Gambling is now thoroughly layered within every community. As the recreation has been recognized for producing profit margins previously unheard of, it's been co-opted by local government and mainstream companies, all queasiness forgotten. The numbers racket, just for an example, used to be a serious crime, left to the purview of mafia types. It is now an important tax boon, overseen by elected officials, its dollars often earmarked for education. A crime? It's a civic duty!

Neither American business nor American government can afford to ignore so much easy money, its cut from the recreational pursuit of better luck. In fact, given its balance sheet and the difficulty in making everybody pay their fair share, our government must do everything possible to exploit our penchant for betting. You might even say it will do everything possible to pervert that residue of recklessness, the trait that settled the country but which now gets burned off under the fluorescence of casino lighting or with the purchase of a few scratch-offs. Go on, do it for the children!

It is just that cynical. Whatever moral or even sensible covenants (not to mention centuries of legislation) there might have been against such a saturation of speculation have been easily overcome in the face of such a bonanza. Gambling has had only a grudging legality, growing over the years but still vulnerable to prosecution even as money floods the Internet in search of a payout. But legal it is, more and more, as government newly defines what's good for us (and it). Sometimes the winking hypocrisy can be fatiguing, as when I discovered a Mississippi "riverboat" (the only condition that allows its operation supposedly being seaworthiness) was moored quite permanently on a concrete foundation (or was until Hurricane Katrina). That "riverboat," which "paddled" up the river to provide a much-needed tourist destination, happened to kick in a good portion of that state's budget in taxes. Sometimes that hypocrisy can simply be infuriating, as when something that used to be prosecuted as numbers running becomes a pseudo-tax. Would we even have public education, if not for states' lotteries?

Look, most of us understand that gambling is not a zero-sum enterprise. The difference between what we take to the table and what we leave with is a function of excitement, the burned calorie, that unit of work that disappears in the pursuit of fun. Most of us agree that it's a fair trade-off. Las Vegas *should* organize the odds in its favor. If it didn't, it would look a lot more like Akron does right now, and what would be the point of our four-day getaway at the Stratosphere?

We usually know what we're getting into. Maybe some Amish kids are getting their lunch handed to them in $5/$10 ring games but the rest of us are less innocent. We're flexing that old muscle, firing up some ancient neurons, trying to remember when the sense of jeopardy wasn't quite so artificial. And we'll pay to do it.

Of course there are some who are mortally aggrieved by the 16 percent hold casinos insist on, or the 50 percent take the states enjoy, or even the 11 percent the neighborhood bookies insist upon. And probably there are instances where the barrier of entry is too low. Now that anybody, of any age, can nudge the line with little more than a mouse click, the opportunity for calamity has presented itself to the very children gambling would help, or so the hysteria of prohibitionists would tell us. Not to discount the ravages of problem gambling, which are genuine. Who hasn't read about the church secretary who embezzled the Sunday collection for her video poker habit?

But, for all the splash such anecdotes make, the risks to individuals are fairly minimal. All the church secretaries with gambling problems have been accounted for by our overworked press. The communities they live in, though, might be another story. When youth hockey is only possible because a gaggle of widows have bingo fever, maybe the problem lies elsewhere. Gambling has become our twenty-first-century bake sale.

The only way to find out for sure was to take my own tour, stopping here and there to pull a slot, play a hand, or pick a number. Anyone who would presume to explain this country is doomed by differences in geography, religion, even weather. I could lose a good chunk of my 401(k) in Las Vegas yet couldn't get a double scotch on the rocks in nearby Salt Lake City. And, yes, they really are both in America. Still, I couldn't help but think there had to be something in our DNA that lured us to the tables, because, obvious differences aside, we all like to gamble and we're all finding ways to do it. Even in Salt Lake City.

Stopping here and there—giving regions representation, giving religions their say, trying to decide how local governments keep their uneasy peace with human nature—also allowed me to experience the astonishing variety of gambling. One day I'm at a meat raffle in the Midwest, the next I'm rattling chips at an Indian reservation in California. Or I'm deciding who wins an Oscar for Best Supporting Actor, or someone else is deciding whether I'll ever draw a pension. Or maybe I'll just push this little button here and predict Whitney Houston will be in rehab by the end of the month.

I did not return from my travels determined to abolish gambling, needless to say. We know what we're doing, if we don't always know why or for whom. We're having fun, mostly. But if we are going to give ourselves over to the thrill of gambling—and that's the way it looks—we ought to know who might be exploiting our ingrown sense of adventure. Who's really sitting across the table from us (Ohio? Phil Hellmuth? Central America?), and are there any cards up his sleeve (the ace of spades, in all cases). Other than that, it's just a matter of recognizing who we really are and where we really live.

This is America, after all, where every day is another

chance to ante up, double down, or pick six. We're a dreamy bunch, always predicting bigger things and better times. We can't help ourselves. Border-to-border and coast-to-coast, we're demonstrating a stubborn optimism, betting on ourselves when we can, on almost anything else when we can't. But always betting.

Las Vegas, Nevada

March Madness, the Mayfield Road Gang, and Statistical Shit Storms

I had never noticed the potential for treachery in an inbounds pass, the inherent calamity in each free throw, the emetic properties of a weakly drafted pick-and-roll. Frankly, I had never paid college basketball the slightest attention at all. They were kids, children really, playing an obviously inferior game, in a vague and poorly predictive incubator for NBA achievement, if anything. As far as I was concerned—not caring that much about the NBA, either—its only attraction was as an agent of nostalgia. An alum might muster interest in his alma mater come March Madness, but it would only be relevant to the extent that there was nothing else on television or his chores on the home front had been completed.

In my own professional travails, first with the *Los Angeles Times* and later with *Sports Illustrated*, I had on occasion been dispatched to cover college basketball, but I found it neither as quaint nor as exciting as my colleagues did. The roost was almost always ruled by a longtime coach whose tenure had come to be confused with color or, worse, character. The game was often boring, the natural effervescence of youth capped by curmudgeonly adults, the whole thing constrained—strangled, I thought—by a geographical and cultural close-mindedness.

Give me boxing, where the human spirit was allowed a freer reign.

Then, for the price of a $110 ticket on North Carolina, I made a remarkable discovery. It was entirely possible that college basketball was the single most exciting and noble game in all of sports, its sluggish back-and-forth really the tactical expression of discipline, the endless passing a symbol for altruism, the five-man weave that was once so tedious now a metaphor for nothing less than democracy. The warm glow I suddenly felt, sitting in a studentlike desk in the Mandalay Bay sports book, may not have been entirely a function of spectacle on the dozen screens hung before me. Probably it helped that North Carolina, favored by two and a half points in the 2005 NCAA Championship against Illinois, had a thirteen-point lead at the half.

So, here we begin, as most people have, in Las Vegas. This is gambling's ground zero, its fertile crescent, where the riotous search for destiny first sprang to life. This has to be the starting line for our race across the country, chasing luck all the way. Where else? Las Vegas is the birthplace of modern gambling, the not-so-little town that was a mythological place long before it was a cheap tourist destination. Now, as institutionalized as it ever was romanticized, it remains the original arbiter of outlaw justice, its ability to sort through losers and winners as unquestioned as ever.

This is where most people come to find out which they are. I was no exception, first arriving here from Ohio in the mid-1970s, passing through on a cross-country trip with my new wife. At that time, the slots and tables were so intimidating the thought of kissing off even a single quarter, even for the fun of it, was simply out of the question. Even though we saw plenty of rubes just like ourselves, we felt dramatically out of place. Our splurge was a milk shake at Caesars Palace's Café Roma, and we expected to get tossed the whole time.

Not too many years after that, I became a frequent visitor, covering boxing for the *Los Angeles Times,* as many as a dozen trips a year, the growing exposure quickly rubbing away at whatever insulation protected my common sense. The frightened hayseed from the 1970s had become Mr. Blackjack himself, discovering an appetite for long odds, tumbling chips of increasingly dangerous denominations across the felt. Looking back, of course, the frequency of my visits had hardly anything to do with my plunge into this netherworld; not a single one of my peers, the guys from newspapers, who made as many trips as I did, or more, ever joined me at the table. It was just me, something about Vegas lighting me up with excitement. There would come a time, after one (or maybe even two) too many trips, when I'd have to come to grips with whatever it was that kept putting me across from the dealer.

And yet, even as my threshold for tomfoolery was increasing, I had never bet on sports. The fact that I hadn't does not call attention to a rigidly defined system of ethics. I truly believe in the right, perhaps even the fundamental drive, to gamble. More than that: I am quite certain that, in the course of performing my duties, I often know more than the betting public. I have seldom been wrong in the prediction of any fight outcome, for example, and can definitely recognize a bad line. Evander Holyfield was not, could never have been, a 42–1 underdog in his first fight with Mike Tyson. That's just absurd.

But I didn't bet on that fight or any other. It wouldn't be professional, or at least not sensible. To cover an event, then return to the keyboard in the wee hours of the morning and face a blank screen, its liquid gases pulsing the demands of a deadline, is an overly choreographed form of torture as it is. If there were other factors at play—the abuse of mortgage money in the absolute certainty that Buster Douglas would retain his title (he gained—holy shit!—how many pounds during training?)—they might compromise the quality, or at least the attitude, of the coverage. In any case, I did not want to be in the position of either lamenting or celebrating an outcome when it was already so hard just to deliver its news.

For the Carolina-Illinois championship game, though, I was a civilian, with no more outside consideration or inside knowledge than the yahoos, nimrods, and rubes beside me. And there were a lot of them, too. It wasn't as crowded—or fractious, I would come to learn—as the first week of March Madness, when the ritual winnowing of a sixty-four-team NCAA field begins in a fevered multiplex environment. That is, by tradition and actual experience, the wildest weekend in Las Vegas. There are four games going at once—a sixteen-game betting buffet the first twelve hours of the tournament alone—and the staggered starts and off-the-wall props provide a nonstop opportunity to find one's destiny in a game between Gonzaga and Texas Tech, two teams you couldn't otherwise locate on a map.

Those are the high holy days for the recreational gambler/ sports fan, hand in hand with the Super Bowl. During that first week of March Madness, it is difficult to find a room in Las Vegas; all 130,000 are booked. And except for the early birds, staking their claims overnight, it's impossible to find a seat in a sports book underneath the winking tote boards and plasma panels. It is definitely pointless to seek any calm, not that you would. It's bedlam. The cheering is specific to each screen and so, as you are watching your own overhead monitor, it can seem spontaneous and bewildering, as if you've been institutionalized in a strange ward that treats unexplained seizures.

You're always looking up, trying to identify the source of your neighbor's tic, as if your hands aren't already full with Bowling Green (which you can't find on a map, either). The conflicting emotions—an expertly made line divides equal parts exhilaration and despair for every possible action—create hallucinatory effects that are not soon washed from your brain. If it's a panorama of apocalyptic excess you want, you could do worse than visit Las Vegas during March Madness.

The actual Final Four weekend is a far less addled affair, as the action is now reduced to just three games over three days, each of them occupying a discrete time slot. There is no longer the necessity to multitask, to juggle lines, to develop life-changing parlays on the fly. The Cinderella teams have gone home, those underdogs that sometimes force the lines-makers into weak numbers and make possible bonanzas for contrary bettors (every once in a while Gonzaga wins—but only in the early rounds), leaving the predicted powerhouse, all of them coached by colorful curmudgeons, their disciplined players the subject of so much office-pool scouting that, for this weekend anyway, the sixth man for Illinois is as exhaustively analyzed as any Super Bowl quarterback. This is serious business now.

What the Final Four lacks in the comparison to the surreal smorgasbord from the first week it makes up for in intensity now that it's all à la carte. It's not as exciting for the pro gamblers, who tend to benefit from big menus, whipsawing the line on an obscure and poorly understood game. They love the early action when teams nobody's ever heard of—"Really," one sports book director asked me, "do you actually know where Gonzaga is?"—are suddenly the topic of everybody's hopes and dreams. The public's natural ignorance, backed by unusual volume (those $20 bets add up in this case), makes their dumb money powerful for just this once, responsible for mouthwatering lines. Plus: "There's a much better chance of putting up a weak number in the first round," he says, "than on an overly analyzed game like, say, the Super Bowl. Or any football game. A game won't run two points in the NFL. In basketball, it could go two-three points very easily."

There is not much whipsawing being done right now. As a goof, I had bet $110 on each of Saturday's games. My money couldn't have been dumber, and so I was lucky to break even, more or less (Caesars Palace, so that their lights might remain on, kept the $10 on my losing bet; that's why it's $110 to win $100). The vigorish, in my case, was the forgivable price of atmosphere, which was one part cigarette smoke, two parts testosterone. I am a steady table player, welcome at several casinos for my blackjack action, and am quite used to the parlor demographic. Lots of young men, sure, but older guys, too. Here in the sports book I was amid a metrosexual mob of epic proportions. They were so alike in youth and carefully groomed appearance—same short, gelled hair; same structured shirts, cuffs loose, tail untucked—that I half expected them to break into a sort of *Queer Eye* syncopation, arm in arm. So this is where every young male goes, right out of college.

Of course, the action is strictly amateur, the outcome nearly beside the point. A sports book during March Madness is as much induction into the adult brotherhood as it is an opportunity to cash a ticket. March Madness is a sort of training wheels for a certain kind of manhood, in which savoir faire can be imputed from such hard-won skills as smoking, the casual wrangling of long necks, and the ability to talk suggestively behind a cocktail waitress's mostly naked back. The level of aggression is quite high and a $22 ticket on the over-under is just one more piece of evidence toward an accurate characterization of Boys Gone Wild. "You would not trifle with someone willing to go that far out on a limb" seems to be the sought-after impression.

Taken as a whole, though, they are not irrelevant. There will be nearly $90 million tumbled through the system—the legal part, the part that we don't wink at. That's about as much as the Super Bowl churns every year. You would lose your mind if you tried to compute the amounts that are wagered illegally, or in office pools (which are legal, providing the host is not scraping off a percentage for his troubles) outside of Las Vegas. Using figures from one federal commission, the total being bet on a season of NCAA basketball might be extrapolated to $19 billion. That's a lot of office pools. To the degree that the tournament exists as an excuse to exercise one's gamble, or just to participate in a community ritual, this goes a long way toward explaining the sport's coast-to-coast popularity, where people can't always place Gonzaga (it's in Spokane; enough about poor Gonzaga) but cheer it all the same.

It also makes the NCAA sound insufferable when it takes off on its antigambling rants. It's understandable that the NCAA would not want its game confused with the lottery, or that it would go a little overboard to insist on the integrity of college basketball. On the other hand, it's a little maddening when the Association pretends there is no relationship between the tournament's popularity and the nation's ability to risk a three-game parlay on Illinois. The NCAA—the self-righteous NCAA—has kept all tournament action out of Oregon as punishment for its *NFL*-based lottery, which would presume to mix sports outcomes with its budgetary bread and butter. Where does the NCAA think its dough is coming from? Try to remember: CBS paid the NCAA $6 billion for the right to televise the tournament for eleven years. Nobody thinks the games are *that* good.

Here in Las Vegas, at least, hypocrisy is pretty much kept to a minimum. Think what you will about gambling's world capital, but this is the most transparent city ever erected. And no matter how it trumpets its mainstream inclinations (would anyone *really* travel to Nevada to see *Avenue Q* for twice what it costs in New York?), no matter how it tries to fit itself into some civic cliché, it's always easy to see right through these social sheers to its true nature. This is a place devilishly devised to kidnap the visitor's sense of propriety, engineered to leverage everybody's lust for bigger and more. Nobody could have set out to design such a fevered dreamscape, setting fantastic mirages upon a pockmarked desert just for the sake of a gorgeous hustle, but in a hundred years of fiscal experiment enough "entrepreneurs" have applied their wits to this unique opportunity and shaped a one-of-a-kind destination, so apart from the rest of the country it might as well require a passport, or maybe even a wormhole, for entry.

There was nothing in its history, or even its geography, to predict its place in our culture. Once known by trailblazing Spaniards as *jornada de muerte*, the valley became a railroad town in 1905 and remained a stopover between Los Angeles and Salt Lake City for the next twenty-five years. When that industry faltered, city fathers took advantage of a recent law legalizing gambling in Nevada and issued six licenses to would-be Wynns. That same year in 1931, the state further liberalized divorce laws so that a six-week stay at a "dude ranch" qualified for residency. And, beginning that same year, construction of nearby Hoover Dam brought in workers and money. It was, arguably, the most important year ever in American tourism, laying the groundwork for an entertainment and economic empire that would surpass everything ever contemplated in the name of relaxation.

The mob, always alert to ancillary income, moved in when veteran bootlegger and hit man Bugsy Siegel, backed by $6 million of old gangland pal Meyer Lansky's Cuban earnings, opened the Flamingo in 1946. The mob had certain skills when it came to games of chance, and the maximizing of profit margins, and it made a good fit for a town that was as wide open as they come. Their mythology made for an illicit attraction, as well, although their tendency to solve disputes outside the court of law might have scared the family trade away. Siegel himself tried to assuage potential customers, saying, famously, "We only kill each other," which was true enough. Barely six months into his operation of the Flamingo, the New York bosses came to believe that Siegel's enterprising ways were at their expense. "Never skim a skimmer" was the lesson here. He was plugged five times—once in the eye, Moe Green–style—while reading a paper in his mistress's Beverly Hills living room, which effectively relieved him of management. For an awful lot of these mobsters, Las Vegas was not merely a metaphorical "journey of death" but the actual end of the line. A hole in the desert was not a figure of speech, either. It was a hole in the desert and usually somebody was in it.

Anybody who's been to Las Vegas in the last twenty-five years can afford to be amused by its past. The casinos are almost all run by public companies, their fortunes merged in Wall Street back rooms, regulated to a fare-thee-well by state agencies. It's not gambling anymore, either; it's "gaming." The mob's gone, replaced by corporations of a certain bloodthirstiness, yes, but which do not, as policy, traffic in genuine gunplay or retire upper management to holes in the desert. Still, that era is recent enough to invoke the thrill of lawlessness, knowingly calibrated for the Midwest rubes who might enjoy a secondhand sense of jeopardy along with the prime-rib buffet. Shopping at the Circus Circus gift shop—the entire casino made real in 1968 by a $43 million loan from the Teamsters, as far as that goes—it's possible to muse upon its original franchisor, "Tony the Ant" Spilotro, who turned the $70,000 concession into a reign of terror as Chicago's enforcer. Spilotro is believed to have put seven colleagues in

holes in the desert and is credited with inspiring the inquisi-
tion scene involving a vise, in the movie *Casino*. He was expert
with an ice pick, too. But no tourist need shudder for the sake
of his safety as he buys a plush toy off the rack; Spilotro hasn't
been seen since 1986. He's in a hole in . . . Indiana, buried
alive in a cornfield, not even the mob was able to look the
other way.

While Las Vegas does not trumpet its defining associations
with the Outfit, the Cleveland Mayfield Road Gang, or even
the Teamsters, it does not distance itself from the unholy
hurly-burly, either. Its rough-and-tumble history is instead a
subtle Chamber of Commerce come-on, its gangland ties a
source of muted mystique. And in case anybody was going to
forget it, what with all the corporate investment in Las Vegas,
in 1999 the city went and elected—by an unfathomable
margin—Spilotro's old lawyer, the happily retro Oscar Goodman, as its mayor and spokesman.

Partly because I wanted to meet a mob mouthpiece, and
partly because I wanted to interview the only city official in this
country with an endorsement contract from Bombay Gin, I
took time out from my March Madness investigation and visited Goodman in his downtown office. Goodman is irrepress-
ible. At sixty-seven, he has a long, ruined mug with a bulbous
nose and is terminally conflicted in what that face is meant
to represent. Half of him wants to trumpet the city's civic
ambitions, its diversification into furniture retailing, the construction of high-rise condominium developments, its high
percentage of churchgoing locals. Certainly he is forward-
enough-looking that one of the exhibits he presents me is a
downtown parcel of sixty-one acres, which he calls the Jewel of
the Desert, an urban village to end all urban villages.

But the other half still wants to talk about the mob. "Best
clients in the world," he says. Like a lot of locals, Goodman
had come here as part of the process of reinvention, traveling

West with a wife and $87 in 1964. He set up his law office in their apartment, operating grandly from a folding card table, and began with bankruptcy cases—$25 per. One of his clients was a pit boss at the Hacienda who, upon completion of a successful insolvency, referred him to a mobster—"alleged mobster," says Goodman, reflexively correcting himself in the retelling—who needed representation for a stepbrother in a stolen-car case. "Kid," he was told, "you're gonna get a phone call and it's a case you better win. Here's three dimes." Goodman had one question: "What's a dime?"

The case seemed unwinnable and Goodman recognized as much. He would like to put a plaque on the courtroom steps where he threw up while trying it. But he did win and from then on became the go-to guy for all of Las Vegas mobsters. "Alleged mobsters," he reminds. "Great guys," he adds, "at least as far as I was concerned, though they did disappear from time to time. What can I tell you?" Like the Ant, the runt killer? Goodman turns serious for a second: "Nobody ever called him that to his face."

Goodman has become the perfect bridge for Las Vegas's past and its future, channeling the guilty fun of the frontier town and rendering it harmless, comical even, for today's high-rise requirements. Perhaps all he's doing is upgrading the mischief. While I was there, the city was trying to close the deliriously seedy Del Mar XXX Movie Motel, saying it was essentially a den of prostitution. The manager, defending every traveler's right to have a place to rest for two hours at a time, said the $35 rate was friendly to more than just the hookers and the johns. "What if you wanted to go and have sex with your wife and you don't want your kids listening while you watch porno with her?" he asked. This appeal was not sufficient to keep the Del Mar open but it wasn't like the hookers and johns had nowhere else to go. In fact, even as this was going on, Goodman was suggesting in a national newsweekly that Las Vegas "may as well be the fastest-growing escort service," and prostitutes ought to be welcome in casinos. The sheets would be cleaner, seemed to be his line of reasoning.

Goodman's war on civic sanctimony is more often waged in the far more suitable spirit of comedy. When I visit him, he had just come back from the Major League Baseball meetings in Anaheim where he'd been campaigning for a big-league team for Las Vegas, and he wants to show me a picture of his presentation. There he is, with an Elvis impersonator and a showgirl on either arm. "Every picture," he says, as if he's noticing this for the first time, "I have showgirls and I'm holding a drink." He thinks for a second more: "Bombay."

On my way out of his office (a reporter from the *Los Angeles Times* is waiting in the lobby for his own media treatment) I hear Goodman call after me: "This is the fastest-growing city in the country, you know." Then: "We're developing an arts center, an academic medical center. It's not all gambling." A little dimmer: "I'm a fun-loving guy. I do everything to excess. I drink to excess, I gamble to excess, I eat to excess. My nature." Finally, as I round a corner, I hear the last of his disembodied voice: "Is that bad?" Mr. *L. A. Times* is scribbling notes like crazy.

I can't tell if Goodman is the last of the breed, a happy-go-lucky museum piece, or if he's still a fair representation of Las Vegas civilization. To be sure, I know others like him, who've come to Las Vegas and, in this strange world of possibility, discovered their true selves. Elsewhere they were misfits, rogues, and outlaws. In Las Vegas they have been able to flower into full citizenship. One of the most successful gamblers in the country—now that he's in Las Vegas—was the worst kind of ne'er-do-well back in Kentucky. A six-figure income in car sales, with even more revenue from a book on the side, was not enough to protect him and his family from a personal and disastrous inclination toward risk. "He had a leak in his game" is what gamblers call it. When people ask what a leak in your game might be, here's one way to describe it: My gambler—whom I'd come to know from my own visits to Las Vegas, and who will enjoy anonymity in these pages, since I can't be sure what's illegal and what's merely embarrassing—once had to have a confab with his wife in the kitchen of their house to say they no longer owned the house that kitchen was in, due to unfortunate properties of math, whereby the casual pitching of nickels—five cents!—had somehow compounded into a real estate transaction.

Through hard work and shrewder gambling, he was, I'm happy to say, able to reverse that particular calamity and restore home ownership to his family. Whereupon it happened again.

After moving to Las Vegas, though, he has become a pillar of society, a major philanthropist, a huge landowner, a political player. He was able to plug those leaks in his game, fall in with more experienced gamblers than him, more properly explore the opportunities the gambling world could afford a man with instincts, ambition, and hard-won management skills. Roulette wheels could be broken (millions won on the mechanical bias of improperly maintained machines), poor sports lines could be wrecked, golfers with insufficient self-awareness could give up a half-million dollars, choking on the same hole, their nose open, day after day. Card games could get destroyed. He once rented a house in Beverly Hills to take advantage of a certain industrial-strength circuit of dubious players. "It was twenty-four hours a day, for months, just brutal," he told me. "But you had to do it." It would have been financially irresponsible not to.

The life my gambler has led has not been without its downsides; he has on several occasions had to find representation with a pre-mayoral Goodman ("A great guy," says Goodman). He's even been dragged from his home in chains, had millions confiscated, and, of course, he's lost money from time to time, as any gambler must. I met with him one fall afternoon and he was casually lamenting his luck over the course of a football season. "Lost $4.3 million last week," he admitted. The way he said it was meant to convey a sense of bewilderment, as in, "Now where did I put my keys?"

He is not a relic by any means, no more than Goodman is. There are plenty more just like him who discover salvation in Las Vegas, their devotion to a life of chance happily accomodated here. But he is less and less visible. As Las Vegas has become more of a real American city than a colony for social outcasts, it is more likely to celebrate the bravado of real estate entrepreneurs like Steve Wynn or Kirk Kerkorian than gamblers like Jack Binion or Billy Baxter. These are the guys who sell the picks and shovels and whose wealth and reputation long outlast the Gold Rush fools who work the sulfurous mines of mathematical possibility. These corporate engineers, who insulate themselves from the vagaries of gambling (gaming; sorry), do not lose $4.3 million a week or get taken away in leg chains. They do not end up in holes in the desert. Boards of directors vote them bonuses when their casinos "play" well.

The mob would be amazed to see their Teamster-funded properties changing hands in corporate boardrooms, sanitized and legitimized so that the Harrah's takeover of Caesars Palace, in a $9 billion deal in 2005, was as important to the U.S. economy as an airline merger would have been. Shenanigans that used to be the purview of a Kefauver investigation are now subject to FTC approval. The Las Vegas gaming industry, after all, has grown too large to be left to amateurs. With more than $33 billion pouring in every year, attention must be paid.

And it is an industry. A gambler can still come to Las

Vegas and make a living, very occasionally a fortune, pecking at the margins of leftover luck, scavenging the remains of poor betting lines, casino promotions, the mind-boggling inflow of would-be Amarillo Slims. But the real heroes these days are the visionaries who understand how to manipulate and finesse and massage the visitors' half-whimsical belief in something-for-nothing. Consider Gary Loveman, the CEO of Harrah Entertainment empire, which now controls about 20 percent of the Strip, including Bugsy's old joint, the Flamingo. Loveman spent most of his career as a Harvard Business School professor, finally attracting notice in the corporate world with papers like "Putting the Service-profit Chain to Work." According to a story I read in *Fortune—Fortune!*—Loveman, who lives outside of Boston, revisits his old PhD papers on retailing for ideas on how best to extract every last dollar from his customers. He looks "at distribution points," is how one analyst put it. Whatever that means. The story also said he used a case study from Taco Bell—which basically was a strategy concentrating on cheap and fast Mexican food—to streamline Harrah's business, which now focuses on lower and more predictable and possibly more loyal rollers. And Harrah's has become a leader in computerizing its clientele, to the point that a customer can be tracked through a casino, through his wins and losses, by a player's card. These particular visitors, by the way, are known to Loveman as AEPs—Avid Experienced Players.

It's hard to imagine that Goodman approves of so much business sophistication brought to bear on his Wild West town but, then, Harrah's stock did rise 50 percent in the year following the announcement of its acquisition of Caesars, making certain people big winners. Loveman was awarded a bonus of $2 million, as well as stock options valued at $5 million. So there's that.

These people, the corporate stiffs who are remaking the

city, may like gaming but the evidence is they don't much care for gambling. Loveman, for example, treats a slot puller as a kind of commodity, something that will regularly and reliably produce a set revenue stream for Harrah's. He disdains the high roller—who can rattle the bottom line with his ups and downs—in favor of small-time but frequent gamblers. This latter group is composed of people who get lured into riverboat and Indian casinos throughout the country and then move up to a Harrah's property. Loveman considers them not gamblers but shoppers. No ups and downs for him.

Even for the new, corporate Las Vegas this kind of hedging is extreme. Everybody knows that Las Vegas was born in risk and has only advanced, however fitfully, with wild fliers. When the city tried to refashion itself as a family destination some twenty years ago, with haunted mansions and log flumes behind casino properties, it lost big. "People come here," explains Goodman, "they want to see Bugsy hiding behind a rock, not Mickey." The city was better suited to the imagination of, say, serial casino owner Steve Wynn, who felt illogical flamboyance—erupting volcanoes and dancing waters—would prevail against family-friendly roller coasters. Indeed, it was just that kind of risk-taking that rescued Las Vegas in the 1980s and made it a must-see stop on the Grand Tour.

The architectural whimsy you see today—the Eiffel Tower visible from the Statue of Liberty, which is not far from the Venice Canal—is an entirely unhinging experience, capable of making a slot machine, with its 92 percent return (would you deposit $100 in your bank account, to withdraw $92 later?), seem like a reasonable investment. The shows within are likewise discombobulating; in one of them, a man sits reading a newspaper, his imperturbability somewhat surprising in that both he and his newspaper are on fire. The show does not have a discernible narrative. A fair question: Is this chaos orchestrated simply to compromise reason in otherwise sensible people? You've seen men in blue paint perform, shouldn't you risk the college fund on the pass line?

Not Steve Wynn, not Gary Loveman, not even Bugsy Siegel could have been so calculating, so diabolical, so familiar with neuroscience to predict the effect of such pointless imagination upon Midwestern tourists. Building a black-glassed pyramid, from which a thematically inconsistent laser beam explodes toward the moon (and which at a certain, magical time of year attracts hordes of moths that, in turn, lure a highly illuminated column of bats; it doesn't get any better than that), would not seem to guarantee visitor satisfaction any more than the water slide that used to be behind the MGM Grand. But there you are; the people behave far more recklessly when they're staying in a scale-model Babylon than they do in a drier, hotter Disneyland. A smorgasbord of sensation, the delivery of ritualized excess, the physical insistence upon confusion is somehow all the groundwork you need lay for the corruption of common sense.

The Strip continues to build out in ways that confound social engineers and, no doubt, the bean counters at corporate headquarters. It is hardly necessary to do a roll call of architectural exaggeration to make the point. When a replica of New York City (complete with a memorial to the city's lost firemen) can do business across the street from a medieval castle, it is no longer possible to apply the normal templates for urban expansion. But if it works—and the bean counters, who, after all, get those State Gaming Control Board reports (We won $1 billion in March? OK!), no longer dispute their designers' ability to inspire greed—it works. When Wynn erected an eponymous casino recently, its particular kind of extravagance being its outlandish cost (how about $2.7 billion?), there was initial concern he had finally miscalculated. Were people really going to book rooms there because a Ferrari/Maserati dealership was on the property? Skeptics soon learned that yes, they would, in the same way they booked rooms at the Bellagio because it had Van Goghs in a lobby gallery. Nobody was going to buy a Ferrari any more than they were going to look at Postimpressionist art during their honeymoon. But it sure is fun to know you could.

Of course there will be a point where supply exceeds demand, when the Ferrari dealer looks forlornly out onto an empty casino, his trade gone to the Bentley guy down the Strip. But that day does not appear nigh. Maybe the hotel-building boom of the 1990s has at least cooled but there was still $6 billion in construction going on as I write this. And why not? There are 35 million people who come every year, leaving behind as much as $12 billion, just gambling, and the numbers grow yearly even as every state but Hawaii and Utah has joined the fray. Or because so many states have joined the fray. A riverboat casino in Illinois is no substitute for a Venice gondola. It's just a form of pre-Vegas grooming.

As Las Vegas grows, and grows ever more outlandish, the proprietors have learned to ensure more and more reliable income streams. Dependence upon gambling, even if it is their raison d'être, is necessary but often frightening. There is no other industry in the world where an SEC filing might note that quarterly profits fell short because a Hong Kong baccarat player had a nice run. At some casinos the high roller is no longer as prized as he used to be; Harrah's Loveman would replace each whale with a hundred minnows if he could. The casino's edge will always play out in the long run (that Hong Kong guy comes back), but it plays out best when the sample is large and predictable.

Room rates are predictable, the price of Dom Perignon is predictable, a ticket price for Cirque de Soleil is predictable. It used to be that gambling accounted for 65 percent of the visitor's budget, but nowadays, thanks to a more realistic pricing of the $2.95 buffet (it's $25 at the Bellagio), it's the food and drink, the room, the show tickets (yikes! $150 to see *KÀ*!), and the shopping that get the lion's share—55 percent. This smoothes out the ups and downs somewhat.

The MGM, which finally ripped out its theme park, has decided to replant the sixty-six-acre parcel with a development of high-rise residences and boutiques. Caesars Palace, which was once vulnerable to wild swings in its bottom line, now operates more like a mall than a casino. Its Forum Shops, a high-end retail space at the end of the casino, is a better bet than any Triple Diamond machine. Nobody at Caesars minds if slots players wander away to fondle the Hermès scarves; per-foot sales there are four times the national average and Caesars gets a nice cut.

Diversification is understandable, now that corporate honchos must answer to stockholders above high rollers. Squeezing profits out of a celebrity chef is easier than counting on a huge drop the night of a big fight. A casino executive once told me it was only with trepidation that his bosses welcomed the high rollers for a big-fight weekend in the first place. "What if they win?" he explained. Well, they probably won't, but just in case they do, the executives can now cash their chips in on a LeRoy Neiman painting in the lobby gift shop.

Still: We're not talking about Broadway here (even if you can see some of the same shows in Las Vegas as in New York) or even Rodeo Drive (although you can certainly buy over-priced jewelry here as well). Las Vegas can never entirely get away—it can't afford to get away—from its original business model, which was to send its visitors home with less money than they arrived. When a gambler leaves Las Vegas, sufficiently fleeced that Steve Wynn can begin thinking of some new sand to develop, about all he takes with him is a sense of having lived a little more fully (and maybe, if he was lucky for once, a Tiffany necklace for his wife, a nice little souvenir). He fired off some neurons he never would back home in Akron, suffered lows and experienced highs he doesn't get at work. The excitement was meaningless but, nevertheless, it was excitement.

Gambling is the thrum of combustion you hear on the casino floor, the bolts of electricity coursing up and down the Strip. It's the glowing vortex you see below you when your $99 charter from Memphis circles for a landing; it sucks you in. It's the gravitational pull that tugs on you, unseen, from across the country, a tidal force. It's an electromagnetic field that rearranges your brain circuitry, a radiation that burns away the protective covering of good intentions, a neural boom that wipes memories clean, erasing the hard drive without disturbing walls or place settings. It's every kind of energy there is, and it will mess you up.

For some it represents a weak force but for others it can be as difficult to resist as gravity itself. If you've ever been to Las Vegas, you know which you are.

Here's me, your personal tour guide across our landscape of luck: A quarter-century ago, it was all I could do to play even the lightest blackjack tables, taking $20 and nervously turning it into a stack of silver. The minimum at most casinos was $2 a hand and if you didn't know to split eights, or watch for tables where the dealer hit a soft seventeen, that stake could disappear pretty quickly. It could disappear pretty quickly, anyway. The $20 represented a day's worth of meals on the expense account and would have to be amortized over the steam tables of some press conference. I didn't like losing $20, but it wasn't the end of the world as long as the fight promoter was willing to wheel out a few canapés poolside.

But—and this is the basic problem/solution to all things gambling—sometimes you win. I won enough, meanwhile learning to split nines against a five, that I was able to steadily increase my tolerance for risk as well as my odds. I soon enough graduated from the $2 tables to the $5 tables and no longer troubled myself about gambling within my expense account. Moreover, I found that if I bet $10 a hand I could avoid the troublesome payoff for a $5 blackjack. I was part of gambling's aristocracy now; I didn't ever have to exchange silver coins again.

And then, over the course of a decade coming to Las Vegas to cover fights, I came to believe I was gambling beneath my station. I was of greater means now, and so removed myself from the dopes who never hit their sixteens against the dealer's ten, or trembled to double-down against his six. I played $25 a hand, joining the elite.

At worst I would lose $500, the most I could get out of an ATM. And mostly I did lose $500, not knowing how to quit when I was ahead. This was not a comfortable feeling but it was not affecting the family budget.

Here's another secret: Inflation works on our greed as surely as it does on our economy. And as soon as I was financially able, I ratcheted my bets to $100 a hand. I noticed that, whatever was going to happen, it now happened quicker and to much greater effect. I might lose $2,000 on a trip to Las Vegas and I might lose it the first hour I got there. But getting on a run, ramping up my bets to take advantage of the inevitable fluctuation within a fifty-fifty game, could produce great piles of chips in just minutes, $5,000 and more. There are people—everybody I knew, now that I think about it— who are invulnerable to that kind of excitement. For them, recreational risk was a low-grade thrill that didn't square with responsibility, let alone arithmetic. But not me. Every time I left, win or lose, I couldn't wait to get back to Las Vegas.

I felt I had finally solved the game, and without learning to count cards or otherwise devote myself to study. It was a matter of discipline. I would bet and bet, waiting for that variation of chance to occur. And it would occur. If you played thousands of hands, as I was doing during a typical five-day trip to cover Mike Tyson or Oscar de la Hoya, you would run into a statistical payback. The casino grind, $100 a hand, could be reversed in a heartbeat. The trick was to endure the grind, which could be horrifying to amateurs. Playing $100 a hand, it was no freak of math to go through $10,000; sometimes it happened the first time you sat down at a table. What you had to do in that case was obvious: You'd go get another $10,000.

The system was bulletproof. It was scary to retreat to the cash machines near the casino cage and run another $10,000 cash advance on a credit card. It was expensive, too; the fee for a transaction like that would easily exceed $600. But for several years, whether playing at the MGM or later the Mandalay Bay, I never failed to recover all investments, and then some. Once at the MGM I had a run of particularly bad luck and exhausted my credit limits on three different cards. The morning I was to return home, down more than $40,000, I had a brainstorm. It never occurred to me that I had "lost" $40,000, only that I didn't have it at the moment. With a frightening calm, I visited a Bank of America branch in Las Vegas and withdrew $20,000 from a home-equity line of credit. This was not easy to do. In fact, I had to go to two different branches to get that much in cash. But back at the MGM I had barely sat down before I won $45,000. Playing $500 a hand, in fact, I must have won everything back in ten minutes. A cashier was kind enough to provide a large shopping bag for its rightful transit back to B of A.

Don't get me wrong, these sums were practically paralyzing and in no way represented a reasonable speculation against my income. I certainly wasn't earning enough to cover a loss like that. Losing $40,000 would have been a crime against my family, which included a wife who was working twice as hard as I ever would, for about a third of my income, and a high-schooler son who had his eye on Santa Clara University, which cost roughly that much a year. But then, I hadn't lost $40,000, now had I? As always, I had won.

Amazingly, my luck held for another year, during which small bags of cash from Las Vegas helped defray that Santa Clara tuition. There were more scares along the way but the winnings were so steady that I feared either or both the MGM and Mandalay Bay would say enough was enough. I was getting comped up the wazoo, plus I was taking their money. How long would they put up with this? I remember telling a colleague, perhaps over a lubricating glass of scotch, that my system was sufficient to pay my son's education. Private school, I added.

The comeuppance was so certain, so deserved, I hardly need explain the circumstances. But some details of it might be of interest, especially if virtual humiliation is your cup of tea. Let's just say, not that long after I'd bragged about my son's "scholarship," I was back at the tables, almost $46,000 down. I was, of course, very nervous, a little embarrassed, but still in action. My original stake of $16,000 had gone quickly, and visits to the cashier's cage at the Mandalay to make my ritual withdrawals might have given me pause as well. I had gotten the same cashier all three times, and her increasingly withering attitude did not encourage me. I was being judged in Las Vegas? But you have to spend money to make money. That's the one thing I'd learned. And here I was, with the final thousand or so, making a monumental run. Had it ever been otherwise? Starting at $500 a hand, I got on a streak and, closing in on my deficit, as always, was pushing $2,000 onto the felt each bet. There won't be any more war stories except just this one: With the dealer showing a five, I was dealt two nines. I split, got another nine, split again until I had four nines. Three of those nines presented doubling opportunities with the second cards, so I now had $14,000 spread all over the table. The odds, I don't have to tell you, were wildly in my favor. Yet, to borrow from Bob Dylan, you did not need a weatherman to see a statistical shit storm brewing.

The pit boss, with whom I had been friendly, gravitated to the action. He was a short, dapper guy, loved talking the fights with me. What I remember is the dealer making his by-now-predictable twenty-one—a blunt-force trauma, all the same—and the pit boss swiveling smoothly on his tiny heels, as if he hadn't seen a thing. For the next twenty minutes the dealer continued to play a game of different-things-that-add-up-to-twenty-one and I was gone, resources exhausted, slightly aghast at the arrogance that produced this result, and also a little hurt. As I gathered myself from the table, trying to execute a dignified departure ("Oh, this? Don't worry about it. I'll take a nap, grab some lunch, probably be back this afternoon"), I remembered thinking, I didn't deserve this.

Whereupon—not even two months later—it happened again.

Now, you're not the queasy sort, or you'd have bailed out on this account several paragraphs ago. So you might be curious as to what happens when a middle-class salaried man, who is saving for retirement, college tuition, and a monumental house renovation, loses nearly $100,000 over the course of a summer. You know why, of course. Now desperate, no longer able to cover up his unreformed stupidity, he made a last stab at squaring his life, fate his only hope. The gambler who refuses to acknowledge losses (they're temporary shortfalls), can hardly be expected to cut them short.

But that's why. Here's what happens. First of all, he doesn't tell anyone. Second, he begins opening those credit applications from banks he'd never heard of, the ones flooding his mailbox with courtesy checks (there is nothing that can't be paid off, given a time frame of geological proportions). Also, he prepares for loans against some retirement accounts, entirely depleting others. There will be enormous tax consequences, of course. Not to mention that he will spend his golden years as a greeter at Wal-Mart. But it can be done, short of declaring bankruptcy or, well, declaring anything. Like I said, first and foremost, secrecy.

Now, one last aside, a final update, to illustrate the surprising flexibility of character that table games—or should I just blame it on Las Vegas?—can inspire. Some months later I was on the road, in Las Vegas, actually, when my wife called, alarmed. She had opened a brokerage statement and seen several withdrawals in increments of $25,000. To my addled mind, the only event unlikelier than losing $100,000 in the first place was Carol opening a piece of mail. And especially a financial statement. She wondered if this was possibly a matter of identity theft; she had recently become interested in the subject, probably because of repeated, overblown reports from Tom Brokaw on the NBC evening news. I had never lied in our marriage but I immediately recognized this was simply because I had never been cornered before. "That absolutely sounds like identity theft," I quickly agreed.

Ten minutes later—she was on a roll of her own back home—she opened a bank statement, showing corresponding deposits, and my cell phone rattled to life on the hotel room desk. What were the odds of her opening two pieces of mail? As far as I was concerned, this was like hitting a superfecta, but in reverse. At this point I was forced to admit repeated failures as a gambler, breadwinner, husband, father, human being. And here is where my luck finally held: She agreed not to divorce me over the phone and, in fact, turned forgiving. It's not something we learned to laugh about, but it never grew to occupy any space in our marriage, either. So, yes, I had made a smart bet somewhere down the line.

And here I was, back in Las Vegas for the Final Four, and with Carol at my side. In the year since, I had dipped my toe back in, gambling-wise. I couldn't help myself, although I had at least learned not to make cash withdrawals on credit cards and had been able to avert further marriage-threatening, six-figure disasters. Carol did not entirely approve, even when I won. Once I pointed out, "You sure didn't mind it when I was buying you pretty frocks," and got a cold look. Still too soon.

She was along this time while I examined the Final Four phenomenon, more or less enjoying the residue of my previous defeats. Dinner at Charley Palmer's had been comped, as well as the room at THEhotel, the all-suites tower at Mandalay Bay that I had helped fund. This was as relaxed a time as we'd ever spent in Las Vegas. Profitable even. Between the two semifinal games, during which Carol retired to the suite to do some work she'd brought along, I even made a quick killing at the same table that offered me those four tantalizing nines, winning $7,500. Returning to the room with my chips, I got at least a smile. I did not trot out my "pretty frock" observation, though.

Carol had to return home Sunday, on account of she had a real job, leaving me to witness the NCAA Final between North Carolina and Illinois alone. I promised to put some money down on the Tar Heels on her behalf, for the fun of it. But that wasn't until Monday night and here I was, $7,500 in chips clacking together in my pocket, and a little bit of time on my hands. Well: I cannot begin to tell you how quickly those chips got out of my pocket. I'm not sure her plane had left the gate before they were gone. Even for someone who had experienced a worst-case scenario, a couple of times at that, the speed of that table-drain was mind-boggling. My plan had been simple: Win back the $100,000 and restore the family finances. And here I was going into the hole again, Mandalay Bay getting ready to break ground for another tower, for all I knew.

My chance for salvation, ridiculous to begin with, was gone. I couldn't learn; all I could do was go broke. With that, oddly, came a kind of peace. There would be several months of waking up, feeling fine at first, and then remembering almost immediately the financial trouble I was in. No getting around that, a slow constriction of my chest every day. But I could hardly get in more trouble, now that all access to money was gone. It was sort of sad to think that whatever money I brought in from now on would be money I worked for—limiting my upside, you might say. But finally I was free of that free-floating anxiety, that inner war of hope and doubt that had produced this shortfall. I was out of business.

Except for that $100 bet on North Carolina. I was surprised to realize how much this mattered to me. The $100—the $110, of course—was not going to be my ticket back to solvency, not even to action, but that hardly mattered. It had become personal. The girl sitting in the student desk next to me had drunk three Sex in the Cities and by halftime was, like me, rooting on the Tar Heels. She'd bet the money line, meaning UNC simply had to win to pay off; she'd get a buck back for every $1.45 she bet. I'd taken the points, meaning I'd win even money, a much better return, but only if UNC won by three points or more. There was no reason to think either of us knew something somebody else didn't. This was a line sharp enough to cut glass and I doubt the smart money was any smarter than mine in this case.

I did remember something a sports book manager had told me, which was always find a reason to like the 'dog. A favorite can attract so much action that occasionally the sports book cannot give enough points away to get action on the underdog. This happens during Super Bowls mostly; who wants to pick against New England? The sports book ends up being a player, unable to offset the New England bets, holding all that Patriot money, hoping for the best. It's the one time of the year they sweat. "The Super Bowl makes or breaks you," the manager told me. But, then, when was the last Super Bowl upset?

But here came halftime, UNC up by 40–27. The girl next to me ordered Sex in the City No. 4 and I vowed (a) to trust my instincts more when it came to sports betting, and (b) find out what is in a Sex in the City. The lead was so great I toyed with the idea of leaving except I didn't really have any place cheaper to go. Anyway, the carnival was fairly intriguing. When the sports book announced second-half wagers, I was astonished to see how many bettors lined up. Were they finding ways to hedge lost bets, or were they just finding a way to double down?

I stayed put and watched with a mounting case of heartburn as Illinois made eight of their first ten shots and got to within three. That was an interesting number, I thought. Illinois faltered, then surged again, tying the score with five and a half minutes to go. With one minute to go, the game was up for grabs, UNC ahead, 72–70. The girl next to me had more bench strength than the Tar Heels for sure; she ordered Sex in the City Nos. 5 and 6. Clearly, she had done this before. Her thinking was, there could be overtime.

It occurred to me that it would be very relaxing to be one of the coaches at this point, at least compared to me. How nice to be untroubled by the spread. All they had to do was win. But I had to consider any number of scenarios, some of them with downright catastrophic outcomes, which were irrelevant to North Carolina. One of them was looming right now: UNC had taken a 75–70 lead with 9.9 seconds left. UNC could not lose. It was not likely to even contest a shot. Even a three-point shot. Which wouldn't trouble UNC fans in the least, but which would turn my little ticket into confetti.

Was there some Illinois player, a cipher in the big picture, who was going to hoist a meaningless three-pointer and thereby become one of those names I'd never forget? No, as it happened, there was not. No sooner had the buzzer sounded, preserving the bankrolls of all us UNC fans, than tremendous lines began forming at the windows. Some of them, like me, were cashing simple win tickets, but many others were turning profits on over-unders, on who made the most three-pointers, on Raymond Felton's point-rebound-assist total. The variety of ways in which a college basketball game could be made interesting was fantastic.

And profitable for others beside me, or even my neighbor, who struggled to get out of her desk, her purse strap tangled hopelessly in the chair leg. I learned later—and this hardly bears reporting—that the biggest winner of all was Las Vegas itself, which recorded its first-ever $1-billion-win month in March. Of that, at least some was provided by the sports books, $16.2 million exactly, during the early rounds of March Madness. The young lads with their long-neck beers and gelled hair may have accounted for additional revenues within the casinos. There may have even been a few other visitors, not so well groomed, who dropped more on the blackjack tables than they won handicapping a bunch of nineteen-year-old kids from Midwestern farm towns. That I couldn't say.

The dilemma for me was how best to present the news of my big win back on the home front. There was no point mentioning that I had dropped $7,500; that development had more or less been revealed in an earlier phone call. By that I mean I had stopped mentioning the triumph. Carol parsed the conversation completely and, in an understanding that nearly broke my heart, allowed the subject to disappear into that sinkhole of marital disappointment. The NCAA Championship win, I felt, was another story. This had been fun, exciting, totally successful. "Our troubles are over," I told her. "We won $100 on North Carolina."

Too soon.

Big Ideas, Flamethrower Money, and Crossing Guards

Anybody who worked at the media company Time Warner, at least in the previous millennium, understands what can happen when huge bets are made in the spirit of corporate omniscience. Not that we were the only employees to see our retirements vanish in button-down hubris, but there is hardly a better example of legal adventuring in the annals of big business. The caper in a nutshell: Somebody thought a $290 billion conglomerate, with venerable and highly profitable businesses, ought to be swallowed whole by a dial-up Internet provider. The times were different in those late 1990s, of course, and anything that had to do with a mouse and modem was seen as a sure thing back in that day. In that go-go environment risk had been completely eliminated by technology. I heard over and over, while watching the ticker on CNBC, that there was a new "paradigm." Still. AOL? AOL was going to buy Time Warner?

It was one thing to lose a fortune as I just had in Las Vegas. I had nobody to blame but myself, and the turn of a card. But what of my punch-in-punch-out job? In Las Vegas I had been irresponsible, no argument there. But in my job, not so much. Yet it turned out that my livelihood was as vulnerable to whimsy as my blackjack stake had been. I was not so naive that I didn't understand that jobs were basically the trickle-down of some higher-up's luck. Every business is a bet won. "I bet there's a market for a mass-produced automobile." But in the modern economy, where adaptability requires one bet after another just to stay in the game ("I bet there's a market for the Edsel"), the gambling can be somewhat less transparent, even as it's more and more necessary. And it can be every bit as dangerous as four split nines.

This was that bet, as reckless a gamble as has ever been made. Most business is an exercise in managing risk. This means taking some from time to time, but otherwise acting as if people's lives depend on every little decision. Here, quite a vast enterprise—the one that had been responsible for my paycheck at *Sports Illustrated*—was put in play on a vague and little-understood notion, a rather farfetched hope actually. Was I about to lose another fortune, on another turn of the card?

I certainly was. And the story of this disappearance was every bit as foolish, not to mention as secretive, as my furtive bumbling in Las Vegas. How this even happened defies understanding. In a company that large, there should have been at least somebody, even one person, to call bullshit on the deal, this crazy merger of two wholly different businesses. Even taking into consideration the high-tech mania that was sweeping the land in the late 1990s, the fever that was leading people to argue online grocers would become the business titans of the twenty-first century (Potbelliedpigs.com was an actual start-up), there might have been somebody in the executive offices at Time Warner who voiced skepticism, who cocked an eyebrow. But no. CEO Gerald Levin, for whom it had been a long time since his Big Idea (HBO), could see no reason why his genius had been exhausted on that single act of brilliance. His enthusiasm for the marriage of old and new was practically evangelical—this was going to be a lot bigger than subscription TV—and the merger was made. At heart, he believed himself a serial transformer of business models.

I guess we all did. Did I say I had been watching the ticker on CNBC? There was nothing so persuasive as a rising market when it came to assigning intelligence, and many a boardroom buffoon was newly diagnosed with Asperger's disorder as stocks doubled, tripled. And yes I watched CNBC, watched my 401(k), fully a third of it in Time Warner stock, soar in anticipation of the deal. Levin and AOL's Steve Case, despite any misgivings I might have had, were looking pretty smart.

And then, scarcely a year later, they weren't. AOL–Time Warner, as it was now known, shed more than four-fifths of its acquisition-crazy worth in the dot.com meltdown, that period of time when common sense cruelly reasserted itself. Levin, who had been shopping for a magazine-cover vineyard in Central California at the peak of this frenzy was soon dogged out of the company and, having ridden the stock all the way down, abandoned plans for an *Architectural Digest* good life (he'd had more houses in that magazine over the years than he'd had big ideas, by a factor of four) and took up a New Age existence in a Marina Del Rey condo, with a new wife. Steve Case steadily cashed options before disengaging himself entirely from the enterprise. Smirking, I imagined. And Time Warner, having eventually recovered some dignity, struck AOL from its corporate hyphenate.

My 401(k) was reduced by two-thirds, this particular idiot watching the stupid stock symbol, whatever it was now, the whole way down. A comfortable retirement at fifty— "flamethrower money," I had warned my editors, only half-joking, of the day I'd show up in the office to take my just revenge—had been replaced by a desperate life of unwanted assignments, an uncertain future. I had a gloomy vision of me and my wife as septuagenarian crossing guards (in addition to my work at Wal-Mart).

Our honchos make big bets all the time, our livelihoods always in the balance. They have to. Businesses often need to reinvent themselves, or at least adjust to changing economies, to survive. Surprisingly, execs crap out at about the same rate as any other degenerate. This is not encouraging. But the history is bleak: Coke was getting killed by the Pepsi Challenge, so struck back with . . . New Coke. IBM was offered the chance to get in on the photocopier industry but said . . . "What's wrong with mimeographs." Xerox, which did seize that moment, later invented the personal computer but . . . passed on its commercial development. Failures of imagination—chips hoarded, cards folded—make lively reading in business books. Caution becomes comical in a history of missed opportunities.

As far as AOL and Time Warner, this wasn't a missed opportunity, just a horrible idea. Somebody went all in without so much as looking at his cards, hoping the flop, some lucky series of events, would somehow make sense of the merger. I can't say that I knew immediately how bad this was going to be (stock symbol, now AOL-TW, going up, up, up!) but I soon guessed there would be trouble. It wasn't so much the way everybody was boasting of "synergy," which in my mind is a kind of executive IQ test (he who insists upon it fails), but the simple fact that Time Warner politely declined to use the AOL e-mail system, preferring the old technology just as it would its old culture. What we had here, as time has proved, just happened to be one of the most reckless, misguided, and disastrous examples of its kind. When these grand ideas pay off—Apple positions itself as a provider of digital entertainment; the iPod is born—it's beautiful. When it doesn't, there are shareholder suits, CEOs disappear to write poetry, and grunts reposition themselves for a longer haul than they ever imagined, assuming they even keep their jobs.

But either way, it's gambling. Any business enterprise is, of course. Without risk, there couldn't be much expectation of a reward. And when you look at it like that—your entire career a roll of somebody else's dice—it can be a little scary. The point is, somebody's always rolling the dice, and you aren't always paying attention. Would you like to quit your secure job at Xerox to be employee No. 3 in a company that just bought, on the cheap, a software program called Quick and Dirty Operating System? Would you like to invest $5 billion in sixty-six low-flying satellites so people can stay connected, worldwide, with a telephone the size of an automobile battery? The difference between cashing options at Microsoft and examining the wreckage at Iridium, that's all. The difference between having "flamethrower money" and none at all.

Business bravado takes a lot of forms and I was reminded recently that it's not always expressed as a roll of the dice, with CEOs bidding for *Forbes* immortality and options out the wazoo, on some half-baked notion. Everyday management is, more often than not, a series of small and unnoticed wagers, each hedged against the other to smooth the bumps of our unpaved economy.

Take Southwest Airlines, a company which, like any other airline, is especially vulnerable to the fluctuating price of oil. In the third quarter of 2005 it bought contracts in the options market on higher oil prices. Don't quite know what that means? It's what every sports bettor does when he pounces on a moving line and "middles" a proposition—getting Notre Dame at −1 *and* +1. In this case Southwest protected itself against the rising cost of fuel for its airplanes by betting other investors in the options markets that fuel would indeed become more expensive. That's a hard bet to lose, at least entirely. If fuel does not get more expensive, and the contracts expire worthless, Southwest can at least console itself that the lower prices will keep operating expenses down, and presumably profits up. It only had to endure the small cost of the options, a tiny price to pay to take some surprises out of a volatile industry. If fuel does go through the roof, as it did in the wake of Hurricane Katrina, then the profits from the options trading will offset higher fuel costs. In this particular quarter, while other airlines were taking a kick in the pants from natural and political upsets, Southwest pocketed $87 million from its hedging to finish the quarter up 28 cents a share. Somebody got a year-end bonus. "Flamethrower money," I'd call it.

At AOL–Time Warner, or whatever it would come to be called, nobody got that lucky. There was a series of financial retrenchments, rounds of layoffs that continue to this day, a stock decline that might have mocked even the force of gravity. AOL, which had presumed to swallow Time Warner with its income stream from subscribers, became a free portal, hoping to survive on advertising. Time Warner, no matter the distance it would try to put between itself and the old dial-up Internet provider, had to sell off assets, even some of its magazine titles. And my retirement was forever deferred, the few stock options I had been granted in place of the year-end bonuses we all got mostly worthless, and my retirement account less than half what it was at the time of the merger.

And what I did in Las Vegas—that was gambling?

Salt Lake City, Utah

The Mormons, Poker, and "Super Good Advice"

Religious doctrine has always been fairly consistent in its opposition to gambling. I've always felt this was not so much a matter of canon as it was a non-compete clause. What other explanation? Because if there's anything more religious than gambling, I don't know what it is.

Consider: Gambling operates on the same principle of faith, whereby fervent hope and correct play is nicely rewarded. Isn't that what religion is? What better way to practice our faith than to bet on the unseen, whether it's a shuffled deck, a random number generator (now there's a holy metaphor if ever there was one), a throw of the dice (more metaphor), or the Lakers (not really a metaphor, except in Los Angeles)? Is there a more perfect expression of a miracle than the last-second field goal that saves the spread? The suck-out on the river? For goodness' sake—for God's sake!—gambling is at the very heart of every religion there is. It might even be the most exaggerated form of it.

As the Latitudinarian theologian said in 1664: "The atheist, as it were, lay a Wager against the Religious man that there is no God; but upon strange inequality and odds; for he ventures his Eternal Interest; whereas the other ventures only the loss of his Lusts."

In other words, it's one thing to bet the mortgage, your 401(k)—as I'd basically been doing—even your life. What I'd been doing was small potatoes. Your afterlife? That's big stuff.

And yet hardly any religion endorses much trust in the supernatural—and we mean this in the most literal sense—beyond its own strictly defined system of spirituality. You can believe in the possibility of God, Allah, Buddha, but probably not in the holy mystery of basic strategy. One or two religions might occasionally exploit the appetite for heavenly deliverance, but only in pursuit of more earthly payoffs. For many years the Catholic Church (which, like Judaism, does not denounce gambling) relied on bingo for fund-raising. There is not a better word, come to think of it, for the manifestation of unlikely hopes and dreams, and the pleasant surprise it produces, than *Bingo!* But outside of that, it's rare to find permission for gambling in any of the scriptures. It's a covetous behavior, grounded in greed, oiled by deceit. Usually a religion is obliged to argue against it.

But no religion has been as effective in the outright deterrence of gambling as the Mormon faith. Salt Lake City, which is the epicenter of Latter Day Saints theology, is probably no more than 50 percent Mormon these days. And that half has grown necessarily tolerant when it comes to accepting the vices of others. That is to say, while caffeine and alcohol remain on the Mormon shit list, a visitor can now find a hazelnut double latte at a Starbucks (which occupies space in a Mormon-owned Marriott!), or even order a once-forbidden cocktail at dinner. There are still a few hoops to jump through; the drinks are so precisely measured—doped out with a pipette that was immediately autoclaved, was my experience—that a single shot of scotch does not seem to even lubricate the ice, and any effort to augment the payload involves maddening complications. When I complained and asked for a double, the waiter advised me—"Funny thing," he said—that such an order would only be possible in the "membership" part of the restaurant.

With that in mind, such ritual enforcement of temperance, you can see why any thesis on gambling must be tested here, under the haloed Wasatch Mountains of Utah, just as surely as it must upon Las Vegas's slightly less rigid sands of Gomorrah. And how interesting that these two states, by the way—the one gambling-centric, the other the only state on the continent to forbid it entirely—are adjacent. If there's truly a Supreme Being, no matter His flabbergasting set of conflicting theories and guidelines, He's at least got a sense of humor.

So of course I would end up here, sooner or later, exploring yet another extreme in our country, teasing out the constants of human behavior from the wildest example of religious conflict not actually in the Middle East. In other words: Exactly how much do we really like to gamble?

A lot. In Utah we learn that human nature is malleable only to a point. Legal, social, and religious constraints might make a dent in gambling activity but they can't quash the impulse to bet altogether. Those strictures just squeeze that behavior on down the highway. So, to that extent, this state becomes a useful workshop in the study of recreational risk-taking. When all opportunity is removed and, further, when the highest legal and moral authorities prescribe rigid guidelines and awful consequences for any gambling, what does a Utah citizen do?

Well, one thing he does: He drives to West Wendover!

It's only an hour and a half from Salt Lake City to the Nevada state line on Interstate 80, a route that first passes the Great Salt Lake itself, and later runs through a salt-rimmed desert. It's an easy ride and thousands of Utahns make it every week. You might wonder why, as you sail into this scorched and briny hell, everything around you arguing against a possible destination, against the likelihood of civilization. But come a final bend, shimmering like a Joseph Smith–style revelation (a sort of pillar of light, not unlike the one that inspired this religion start-up), is a five-casino outpost, absurd in its neon insistence upon entertainment, here of all places.

West Wendover, Nevada, has nothing going for it but the accident of geography, which makes it the point of Nevada closest to Salt Lake City. Studies show that a fourth of all adult Utahns travel here to gamble each year, that more than 40 percent have gambled here. That, furthermore, they've dropped nearly a quarter-billion dollars, which are used to light up this corner of the desert, to satisfy Harrah's stockholders, to school Nevada's children. If West Wendover is an experiment in the effects of religion upon human behavior, you would have to conclude, at the very least, that official doctrine travels to the state line and no farther.

There can be no question that Utah and the religion that supports almost all its legislation have only made gambling inconvenient. Not undesirable, and certainly not impossible. Salt Lake City's *Deseret Morning News*, looking into this in 2005, found that the top six Idaho lottery sales, out of nearly twelve hundred stores, were on Utah's border. It found that the Kwik Stop, just north of the border on Interstate 15, sold $2.54 million in lottery tickets in 2004. That's twenty-seven times the average of all other Idaho locations. In all, Utahns have so far contributed about $23 million to Idaho's education and building funds.

But in spite of the prevailing social and moral circumstances that inspire Utah gamblers to take regular trips to nearby states to indulge their habits, even in Salt Lake City, it's possible—difficult but possible—to find ways to experience the thrill of gambling. Just as the local mores force you to reconsider the symptoms of alcoholism every time you order a cocktail with dinner (a double! Good Lord!), so does the unnatural effort required to gamble prove your degeneracy.

There's a lot of bingo going on, for one thing, but you really have to want to play bingo to go through this. The dreariest excuse for a gambling den that I saw was the Fast Action Internet Café & Bingo, which was hidden away in a strip mall on a main drag about a mile or so south of Temple Square. There, in two claustrophobic rooms, you could buy "Internet time" and sit at one of a dozen or so computers and e-mail the grandkids. Or, as all of the old-timers were doing on my visit, swallow your shame and play full-fledged video poker and hope to pick up that $1,000 payout before Social Security runs out. I'd have sooner been spotted in an adult video arcade (which Utah definitely does not have).

This truly was a religious effect, which as ever was simply intended to make you feel a little bit worse about yourself as you went about obeying human nature. Gambling was happening, as God must have intended, but it was now at the risk of sanction and embarrassment. Or of highway driving. Well done, Latter Day Saints!

What I wondered, though, was how religion might impact poker, which had been lately working its way through this country like an auto-virus, a recreational worm that had been infecting everybody's hard drive. I could see where the Mormon faith, in conjunction with state and local government, could tamp down bingo parlors or otherwise outlaw casinos. But could it contend with poker, which, like sex, was conducted in the privacy of homes and, apparently, with the same approximate regularity?

Let me give you a taste of how far-reaching poker is, and what the Mormon religion is up against: In one week during July, which, admittedly, was the beginning of the 2005 World Series of Poker, I watched as this country became all poker, all the time. I couldn't get away from it, nobody could. This particular week there was going to be more than a hundred hours of poker on TV, a broadcast phenomenon which had already been flogged to death in the press (I had written about it nearly two years before) but which was still real enough that the pioneering producer—the World Poker Tour first turned it into a spectator event with the use of the card cam—had just gone public. It remained so real that, during this same week, a group supposedly fronted by legendary player Doyle Brunson was offering $700 million to buy it.

Anybody predicting deflation of this fad was bound to be confounded. And it was certainly reasonable to call a poker bubble these days. I was reminded that *Who Wants to Be a Millionaire* was a good idea, too, until it finally dominated the schedule and Regis Philbin became the face of prime-time TV. When "Is that your final answer?" turned into a national mantra, even ABC knew it was time to pull the plug on a tricked-up game show. I suspected the poker craze, at least as it was represented on TV, was in a similar end-stage when, that same week, I tuned into Celebrity Poker Showdown and saw Malcolm-Jamal Warner move all-in against Fred Willard.

There were other signs of a market top. Not only was the *New York Times* covering the WSOP, it had—just that week— instituted a weekly poker column. The *Wall Street Journal* had weighed in with reviews of a number of poker books. And there were a lot of them, by the way. A scroll through Amazon demonstrated the growing preoccupation; the available library had grown so vast and so literate that it constituted a self-help genre more than an instructional one. *Harrington on Hold 'Em* was now beating out *The Purpose-driven Life*.

My own magazine, *Sports Illustrated*, had recently run a lengthy piece on Internet poker and the awakening of the youth market. And ESPN (which had thrown in its lot with the WSOP several years before) was bragging that its tournament coverage had higher ratings than everything but NFL and NASCAR. Accordingly, it was cutting the "sport" up in about a dozen different synergistic ways. And I forget, when did poker become a sport?

For added emphasis, the *New York Times Sunday Maga-*

zine had, the week before, profiled the agreeable poker maniac Daniel Negreanu (his "mommy" packs his tournament lunch in Tupperware). And then—the same week that I'm talking about—*The New Yorker* landed on my doorstep with a six-page story on some Texas hold 'em misfits (damn you, Negreanu!) who were becoming multimedia franchises, as well as national celebrities.

As I said, it was tempting to call it a craze, to predict a collapse that was as obvious as the ultimate failure of Pets.com should have been. A cover story in *Time* would be the abandonship indicator ("Poker: The New National Pastime"), as usual, the signal to move on to the next cultural trend. Any day now.

And yet . . . poker just kept rolling on, getting bigger, as if the combination of TV exposure and Internet access was transforming an ancient card game into a national amusement. It's true, there are hardly any recreations more thoroughly American than poker, a frontier game devoted to the principles of mischief and luck, refined during the Civil War and part of our national personality ever since. But it's always been a niche hobby, acceptable yet hardly the platform for coast-to-course conversation. It was much more like jazz than like baseball. What was happening now, this was something else.

I suspected the residual romance of the game had a lot to do with its new popularity. You go back in our history and you have Harry Truman mulling the use of a vaporizing A-bomb while playing cards with the press. But the game resonates most as a reckless and willful assault on convention, almost always illegal and often enough deadly. No doubt today's online player derives at least a small frisson of apprehension when he draws aces and eights—the last pairs Wild Bill Hickok ever looked at. The likelihood of the Dead Man's Hand actually producing mortality is extremely remote these days, especially online, but the historical subtext has to add some nervous excitement to a dialed-up game of Chutes and Ladders. Anybody ever shot dead at contract bridge?

In fact, all our pastimes are pretty safe and it has become more and more difficult to work off our manly impulses toward self-destruction and self-aggrandizement. Very few of us care to do what it takes to win a Formula One race or scale the Eiger, but a $1/$2 home game is not out of the question. It's not especially dangerous anymore but it still feels a little illicit. And the exchange of money, made possible by the slightly disturbing wit that poker requires, satisfies the rascal in all of us.

Poker poobahs recognize this appeal and have been careful not to legitimize the game beyond its original fascination. They don't want to find players with aces up their sleeves, but they don't want to make it family fun, either. Properly enjoyed, the game should forever be wreathed in the ambient smoke of a mythical frontier.

T. J. Cloutier, an ex–football player whose gruff hulk has graced many a final table, bridges that chasm in poker history, the divide between a life of dangerous piracy and that of visiting professor. Cloutier is a best-selling author, like any respectable poker pro these days, and enjoys a reputation as the greatest tournament player of all time (despite never winning the WSOP). But when he started his poker career forty years ago, having folded his life as derrick man in the Texas oil fields for more reliable strikes at the Brass Rail, poker was hardly the antiseptic sport we watch on the Travel Channel now. As one of a corps of Texas road gamblers, Cloutier regularly "faded the white line," showing up at shrimp shops in the bayou, traveling to Odessa, Waxahachie, San Angelo—anywhere there was a game. It was not a particularly calming line of work, although it did generate a colorful vernacular. "In those days," he told me, "the first thing you had to do was keep the cheat off you." Gunplay was not out of the question, holdups always a prospect, and a fair game was a pie-in-the-sky proposition.

"I showed up at this joint outside of Baton Rouge," he told me, "knocked on a door, looked through a peephole and said I'd heard there was a game. Somebody, other side of the peephole, said, maybe, and was getting ready to let me in. I said, 'Now, is this the type of game where if I win, I can get out again?' This guy—big guy—thought for a second. I don't think anybody had ever put it to him like that. He said, 'Could I suggest you play elsewhere?' "

Doyle Brunson, forever nicknamed Dolly after a writer's dyslexic accounting of his legend, is another old-timer whose poker longevity has allowed him to straddle the gap in its history. He fronts a Web site, still wins tournaments (he won his tenth WSOP bracelet in 2005), is a fixture at the Bellagio's high-stakes game, and remains poker's best-selling author (his twenty-five-year-old *Super System* still sells ten thousand copies a month). Yet he's also fluent in old-timey rounder talk and is always the go-to guy for writers looking to color up their otherwise dry reporting of hands played, chips won. At the 2005 WSOP, where the seventy-one-year-old Texan was discovered by the *New York Times*, he rehashed an old favorite to great response, an anecdote of an Austin hijacking that featured shotguns, dropped drawers, the promise of a spot-check, and the possibility of blown-off legs. Brunson, in his syrupy drawl, recalled that the half-naked players were in a panic to remember just where it was they had squirreled their money away. "Oh wait, don't forget this $400."

But if the Brunsons and Cloutiers remain relevant, it's only because of their ability to recall an outlaw game, a game that hasn't really existed for some time now. These days the stars—and they are stars, thanks to the WPT and the WSOP broadcasts—are comparative kids, math freaks, dot.com dropouts, super-staked amateurs, college kids just coming off the Internet incubators. Few, if any, have ever sat in a backroom poker game and seen the player next to them get his head blown clean off (Brunson again; keep 'em coming, Doyle). For the most part they don't even have to worry about being legal. There are aboveboard card rooms throughout the country, a broadband connection in every home, and flights to Las Vegas on the hour. And when is the last time you heard of a home game busted, raided, or otherwise hijacked?

That's not to say there are any fewer characters, just that they are more likely to die of natural causes. When the WPT first got going, I went to the Bicycle Club in Los Angeles to visit with some of them during a tournament stop. Cloutier was there, as well as some high-level amateur-geezers like Bob Stupak (the guy who gave us the Stratosphere in Las Vegas) and Lakers owner Jerry Buss. Mostly, though, it was represented by the new breed, smart guys with misplaced work ethics who simply could not believe there was this much dead money coming their way.

The WPT, with its introduction of the card cam, had been a huge boost. Beginning in 2003, the outfit struck an alliance with the Travel Channel and began broadcasting high-stakes Texas hold 'em on a weekly basis. The effect was galvanizing. The game, "the Cadillac of poker," as TV host Mike Sexton reminds us before every show, makes *Who Wants to Be a Millionaire* seem complicated. No offense to the purists, the players who make their livings decoding nervous tics, or the viewers who flood chat rooms to parse every check-raise, but Texas hold 'em is basically a game of chicken. The simplicity is overwhelming. The player with the most chips bullies the others into a Wild West showdown, some desperado pushing his chips all-in, the two gunslingers immediately rising from their seats to watch the dealer mete out their destiny below them. Fate haunts every hand.

What makes it such good TV though is not the combustion of wishful thinking, two guys (or, occasionally, gals) mistaking hope for a cosmic obligation, or even that pornographic money shot when the ex–*Playboy* centerfold spills $1 million in cash onto the table for head-to-head play. It's that wicked card cam, which reveals genius or idiocy, caution or arrogance, in every hand. Every televised tournament since has latched on to the idea, showing the two hole cards, giving the viewer the same omniscience every player already assumes, or pretends. The really smart player can examine the betting, his opponent's reaction to the flop, and "put him on" a hand. Well, he thinks he can. But we really do know that our hero, greedily slow-playing his Siegfried and Roy, is actually marching directly into the immutable jaws of probability—his opponent's made flush. Ooh, how delicious to see such hubris punished! And from the comfort of our couch.

Such drama not only inspired viewership (and created one knockoff after another) but drove ordinary, nonrogue mortals to this outlaw game. Internet poker rooms were proliferating to accommodate the influx, people so innocent of the perils of online piracy (for all they knew, they could be sitting down next to Brunson, a 'bot, or some computerized buccaneer with a boiler-room operation playing all five hands against them) they were willing to ante up for a relatively inexpensive education.

The Internet, with thousands of online rooms and who knows how many ring games, offered an incredibly accelerated curriculum. Poor Brunson, aside from worrying about buckshot patterns, could never in all his years accumulate the kind of experience these Internet kids can get in even a few weeks. In the time it took him to find a game on "Bloodthirsty Highway" in Fort Worth (again, Doyle, obliged), any cyber-rounder can play thousands of hands. This sort of hermetic experience, which is absent the human give-and-take of the home game, was initially discounted. How can you learn to read your opponent, sense a bluff, recognize a tell when you're staring at desktop icons? Maybe you can't. But maybe it doesn't matter.

In what became a seminal event in the history of poker, the aptly named Chris Moneymaker won the 2003 WSOP, all $2.5 million of it, never having played a single hand in a smoke-filled room. An accountant with a bit of a gambling jones, he'd learned the niceties and even earned his WSOP buy-in playing in an online room. As one newbie after another claimed spots at final tables, it was fair to ask, what niceties exactly?

There must have been some; the top players still dominated over the long run. But Moneymaker's success surely demystified the game and encouraged a lot of people to confuse luck with skill. And, really, in a game that depends almost entirely on the turn of a card, is there that much of a difference? Participation soared (almost 60 percent from 2005 to 2006), prize money ballooned, and everybody who understood the distinction between pot roast and pot odds was turning professional. At the 2006 WSOP there were 8,773 entrants and a pot of $82.5 million, ensuring that anybody who made the final table would win at least $2.8 million (the winner, Jamie Gold, left Las Vegas with $12 million, roughly twelve times what Chris "Jesus" Ferguson won in 2000 and almost five times what Moneymaker won just three years earlier).

The poker boom, which was drawing everyone in, from patent attorney (2004 WSOP winner Greg Raymer, another Internet qualifier) to celebrity (Ben Affleck even won a small tournament) to celebrity wrangler (Gold had been an agent for folks like James Gandolfini and Jennifer Lopez), may have mainstreamed the game beyond any recognition. When one-time beauty queens get written up in the Style section of the

New York Times for their hold 'em play, well, we're not talking about a frontier game anymore, are we? Poker was becoming an economy unto itself, legitimate and respectable, the stuff of IPOs and other corporate shenanigans. The players I talked to were more worried about "branding" and "income streams" than getting out of town with their bankroll.

The game still self-selected for oddballs with astounding high-risk tolerances. The gallery I ran across, for all the collective education and work experience, was still decidedly misfit-centric, verging on nuts. Phil Laak, when I first met him in 2003, was playing cards in wraparound shades and a hooded sweatshirt and was known, predictably, as the Unabomber. He was good-natured about the tag, as you might have expected of someone who had never actually heard of the real Unabomber. "I'm that guy?" he asked me, in genuine surprise. He was reluctant to give me his age, as he believed in the power of mystery. He said he learned the game in underground clubs in New York and, at the moment, was plying his trade in Northern California. He further told me he was "super" risk-averse, considered the $5,000 buy-in for the Bicycle Club tournament to be a "fat chunk of dough," and was always on the lookout for "actionauts, guys from outer space who juice it up with their game theory." Also POWs (Pay Off Wizards) and GWIDs (Genius Wizards in Disguise). Later on, I saw he was dating actress Jennifer Tilly and was hosting a *Cribs*-meets-*Rounders* TV show on the E! Network, called *Hollywood Home Game*. He would knock on a celebrity's door, say one of the costars of *That 70s Show*, look into their refrigerator, and then give poker tips.

At that same tournament I met Chris Ferguson, whose long black hair had given him the nickname Jesus, somewhat fudging the resemblance unless Christ really did wear a cowboy hat, reflecting shades, and pointy boots. Which reminds me: The one thing I learned about poker is that if you look like someone, you will be named for him, without any possible allowance for irony or good taste. A player with a certain kind of mustache would be Adolph the rest of his life. Ferguson, besides being a WSOP winner and a top-celestial look-alike, had a lot going for him. He could cut pieces of fruit with a thrown card and once won a swing-dance competition in the Jack & Jill division (brother-sister). Also: He had a PhD in artificial intelligence from UCLA, a subject he spent some little time trying to explain to me. "Never mind," he finally said. When I asked why he would study artificial intelligence, he became flustered. "Why wouldn't you?" he countered.

Closer to the stereotype, updated only somewhat, was Gus Hansen, an anything-but-melancholy Dane who is known on the poker circuit for his aggressive play. Crazy play, actually. He gives the appearance of betting randomly, as if he recognizes the foolishness of relying on such incomplete information as two miserable hole cards. And yet, or perhaps consequently, he is a terror on the WPT circuit, making final table after final table, running up tournament winnings of more than $1.5 million at one point. When I spoke with him he was still in the process of smoothing out his game, although it seemed to me that poker was the least of his worries.

He told me he had recently built up a stake of $500,000 playing in underground poker and gin rummy games in New York but, in a wild two-week spree, had given it all back in Russian card games. "It was hard getting to sleep the first couple of nights," he said of the debacle. Well, of course. My question: What in the hell are Russian card games?

Going broke, from time to time, is part of the deal. Almost all the poker players I spoke with realize that particular inevitability, a doom all the more certain for their utter lack of discipline. Never mind the vagaries of flipped cards, where mathematical intuition is all too often revealed for a bad guess. These guys have a tendency to bet even outside that vague expertise. Hansen told me it can get kind of crazy, all the recreational prop-betting among them, and that even he was amazed to find himself involved in a complicated parlay of athletic feats that required him to dunk a basketball with $50,000 at stake. "I'm a terrible jumper," he confessed. Fortunes won on the felt are easily forgiven on the greens, at the sports book, online, in wild-ass opinions on an airliner's ETA.

Of course, it's always been easy to go dry just playing poker, never mind having to predict what the new Batman movie will open at. Even Phil Hellmuth, a talented player who has become as famous for his bad table manners as his hold-'em action, has gone "cash-broke" a number of times. This, the most recent time, was not in the foolish flush of a beginner's career, but rather long after he'd won two WSOPs and authored poker books and been featured as the WPT's resident brat. Hellmuth, who owned several houses at the time ("cash-broke, not broke," he told me), was not overly concerned, saying, "I had an overwhelming sense that I'd be taken care of." That's the gambler's mind-set for you; he truly believes the universe favors the risk-taker. Hellmuth was somewhat reassured that if things went any further south, he could at least find somebody to stake him. So there is always that. Still: Newly married the first time he flatlined, he remembered being more irritated than worried. "The bills," he said, "they seemed annoying to me during that period. That's all I remember."

But these days it's becoming impossible to go broke. The players still hustle side games, still suffer setbacks at craps, and occasionally lose concentration when challenged to guess each other's weight, $10,000 a pound. They behave dangerously, as always. Not so dangerously, though, that they can entirely demolish the advantage this poker boom has created for them. Deep-money tournaments, where a $5,000 buy-in can produce a $1 million payday. "Running a toothpick into a lumberyard," Amarillo Slim used to say. Stationary targets, millions of amateurs graduated from the online rooms, who treat these tournaments like a fantasy camp, happy to give their money away just for the heady experience of going heads-up against Phil Ivey. It's just too rich, too easy.

Hellmuth can hardly get over it. Not only are the tournaments worth more than ever—and more of them, too—but the field is easier to wade through. It's true, the sheer size of a tournament, requiring so many more hands to reach a final table, is bound to make it more difficult for any one pro to dominate. But the greater sampling also restores a mathematical order, reducing the effect of bad beats, where wit and nerve are all too often voided by runner-runner. It's a little less random.

More than that, the craze is making businessmen out of these rogues, legitimizing them right into full economic citizenship. Forget the tournaments, even though almost all of the WPT stops offer a first prize greater than $1 million. These are life-changers all right, but also, as in golf tournaments, platforms for further wealth-building. Hellmuth bragged to me that his first book, *Play Poker Like the Pros*, had nearly a hundred thousand copies in print and he was negotiating another contract, for a follow-up. He walked away from an infomercial, thinking he could raise the $750,000 offer to $1 million (he couldn't; late-night pitchmen are harder to bluff than his customary riffraff). He was upset about that. But there's always Poker Nites, lending himself out at $10,000 a pop when times are bad and, of course, online poker—"telecommuting," he calls it.

Hellmuth may have been a little more than full of himself, talking of "multiple income streams" and "branding," but he was not far wrong in imagining a future where former World Series champs would have their own bobblehead dolls. Thanks to the online sites, many of the digital generation have richer endorsement contracts than do baseball players. Negreanu, in a now-obvious move, has partnered with Viacom on an Xbox poker game. And even an analog fogy like Cloutier finds a way to participate. Last I heard, he was sailing the seven seas, resident crab on a poker cruise.

Well, maybe this was our new national pastime after all. The democracy of poker, imposed by a simple shuffle of cards and easily grasped rules, was so inviting that hobbyists, college kids, and office workers with a T1 connection and time to kill were all competing on a more or less equal footing with the hardened cases who actually make their livings at this. Just as pros can tumble into an abyss of arrogance, mistaking their science of incomplete knowledge for a mastery of the universe (and lose), so do the amateurs occasionally ascend those same slippery slopes of probability (and win). The assumed prerequisites of experience, Mensa-type math abilities, and other articles of magic could be easily voided by pocket rockets.

If not a pastime, surely a phenomenon, and it inevitably reached even the most unlikely of places: Utah. Suddenly card rooms were springing up everywhere and many of them took the nationwide acknowledgment of the game as an unspoken permission, even here. Would-be poker moguls, kids usually, advertised tournaments brazenly, on the Internet and in the alternative newspapers. There were local news stories about college kids taking it up, about WPT whizzes who happened to be from Salt Lake City, about the proliferation of organized games.

It was, in short, too much. At a general conference in April 2005, the current prophet of the LDS Church, ninety-five-year-old Gordon Hinckley, was moved to take poker head-on. Although, as any prophet, Hinckley is subject to revelations (such as a reversal on polygamy that was beamed down in 1890), this address was not the stuff of miracle but Mormon common sense. At the conference Hinckley recounted some anecdotes expressing poker's popularity and the possibility it was a kind of gateway drug to gambling addiction. "From the letters I have received from members of the Church, it becomes apparent that some of our young people start by playing poker," he said. "They get the taste of getting something for nothing, and then travel outside of the state to where they can gamble legally." No good.

Hinckley rattled off the Church's historical opposition to gambling—that damned getting something without honest effort—and renewed its stance, especially as it related to poker's persistent popularity: "If you have never been involved in poker games or other forms of gambling, don't start. If you are involved, then quit now while you can do so."

Whatever you might say of Hinckley, he is not vague. His comments were not "manifesto" quality, and Mormons I talked to believed they were more in the spirit of lifestyle guidance, of preserving mental and economic health than religious law. One religiously conflicted rounder I spoke to simply took it as advice, to be followed or not. The real test, as far as he was concerned, was whether a poker player, having admitted his gaming in the ritual premarriage interview, could still enjoy a church wedding. He was sure that was still possible.

All the same, it was interesting how quickly authorities began tightening up what had been a loose ship. One fellow I talked to, who had been operating a home game, advertising even, said he began noticing "cops on the curb" during poker night, chilling roll-bys. A friend who had connections in high places advised him to shut down. He did. Other "clubs," which offered "prizes" for points and operated quasi-legally, were closed very soon after Hinckley's address. A community education course on Texas hold 'em was quickly canceled. A Web site that used to list dozens of home games in Utah now lists none.

One person who operated on the fringes of the poker

community in Salt Lake City said it wasn't as if Hinckley had brought some tablets down from a mountain, and that not all Mormons practiced the faith flawlessly anyway. "Plus," he said, "there's a lot of 'Jack' Mormons, people who are Mormon but still do their thing." Still, he was surprised at the initial effect of Hinckley's comments. "A lot of people," he said, "seemed to regard it as super-good advice."

But poker had become too popular to go down without a fight and, anyway, it had survived manifestos, legislation, and moral disapproval before. The Mormons were mighty effective when it came to regulating human behaviors that, elsewhere, resisted modification but . . . poker! This was going to be tough. Or, to judge from the vaguely illicit activity that was continuing to flourish in the Utah underworld, and which I easily gained access to, impossible.

Pedro, who ran one of the most successful underground card rooms (all names and some identifying details have been changed), was my eager guide. He was not so much a religious reformer as he was a proud entrepreneur, making some money at it but also elevating the scene above its ritual shabbiness. Before he allowed me to see his club, he conducted a tour of some of the others in the city and I was struck by the determined crumminess of each of them. They were in decrepit residential neighborhoods, industrial zones, warehouse districts—in areas that, as grim as they were in the light of day, no doubt crawled with dope fiends, carjackers, and opportunistic rapists past midnight. As I say, there was almost something purposeful about the dilapidation, as if these hyper-scary spook joints only heightened the below-board poker experience. We're all here to take a chance, right?

That night at Pedro's game, though, I had no reason to fear for my life. It was in a small commercial building about two blocks off the main drag, with its own fenced-in parking lot. A local Ultimate Fighting star—the city seemed to be a UFC hub, for some reason—worked the back door, buzzing in the regulars. Up front, a wise-guy bail bondsman, at least legally the building's principal tenant, stood distracted watch from his glassed-in outpost. I couldn't tell for sure if he was just one more layer of security or comic relief. He was a twenty-something guy in flip-flops, sweats, and a backward ball cap. While I was there, he devoted more time to fine-tuning his fantasy football roster than to responding to clients. Every once in a while he'd drift back from his office, bump knuckles with a player, or even sit in on a few hands. "Life of a bounty hunter," he explained.

The setup was more like a basement rec room, really, which makes sense, because that's pretty much its genesis. Pedro had been running a game out of his own home, then in a decrepit house with a partner, then a hyper-scary spook joint in a warehouse district by himself. In the three years he'd been doing this he came to see that the younger players did not absolutely require the secondhand smoke of jeopardy. More than a near-death experience, they wanted a safe game, a room with a beer machine, three televisions, a couch in a dark corner for that six a.m. nap, and a host who would "book" you occasionally and always order out. Pedro is a big, goateed thirtyish guy who, for all his forbidding appearance, is surprisingly sweet-natured. This counts for something, too. His game has its raffish element but the overall tenor is decidedly non-threatening. It's a friendly place to play poker.

Pedro explained to me that his sideline—he works in employee risk management during the day ("Irony, huh?")—is not without concerns. Although his patrons don't have to worry unduly about getting hijacked, stiffed, or arrested, he does. In his case, the concerns aren't huge. None of the games—there are seven others in town—have been taken down for ages. In the last ten years there was only one robbery, when masked invaders interrupted Larry's game (in a decrepit house), asked for Larry himself, and walked out with a nice pot. In that same time, there's only been one sting. Authorities acknowledge these games are illegal but likewise admit they're not going to invest undercover work in something that's going to result in a Class-B-misdemeanor conviction. Plus, who could possibly care?

More immediate worries are competition. It was up to Pedro, the relative new kid on the block, to carve out his own niche in the local business community. Part of that was the decision to run a relaxed game, not a Wild West shooting gallery. But as refined as the amenities were—as nice as the new twelve-handed table, the clay chips, the huge trays of pasta and sausage from a nearby Olive Garden, the implied security— his real marketing genius was the decision to offer no-limit Texas hold 'em, only. This had become the game of choice among younger players, schooled on World Series of Poker and World Poker Tournament broadcasts. The other games in town had been slow to recognize the change and were stuck with an older and naturally dwindling clientele. And now Pedro was gaining players almost faster than he could accommodate them.

At the moment, he was running games three times a week, plus a Saturday tournament, sometimes three tables at a time, the players arriving almost as fast as a UFC bouncer could buzz them in. He was already subletting one of the nights— he still had a regular job, after all—and was considering doing another. It was crazy. Somebody was always calling him, wanting to know if friends could join the game. Strangers popped up at the door, offered bonafides, and waited along the wall until a seat opened.

Pedro, whose lifestyle included big trucks and strip clubs, was making a killing. His dealer (who can make up to $650 in tips a night, for that matter) raked up to $4 out of each pot, and there were probably twenty an hour. And there were often twelve such hours a night. Pedro said he probably put $2,000 in cash in his home safe each week, some of which went directly to lap dances and car payments, but not all of it. So, yes, hold 'em.

But even that doesn't fully validate his business model. Pedro must overcome an additional hurdle, one that ought to be fatal to any poker start-up. It's one thing to run an underground game, to worry about the law, about customers you've "booked" who disappear and never pay up, about other operators poaching your players. Civil codes and aggressive business practices are the least of his concerns. At his game, most of his players must acknowledge their sinning as soon as they ante up.

The ones who don't, among the Mormons bellying up to Pedro's table, at least regard it as guilt-inducing, but seem to have made their peace with the religious conflict. A twenty-something player told me he struggled with the Church's stance but he felt poker, with its emphasis on skill, was a special situation, without a total reliance on luck. "My mom," he told me, "she's a day-trader. She throws money in, something happens. I don't quite understand the difference. My brother-in-law, he lost everything in his business, his whole life, in five or ten minutes."

Pedro told me that maybe a third of his players were Mormon. Indeed, a partner who ran his Wednesday-night game was a Church member. Pedro said he had just lost one of his best young players; the kid was leaving that week for his mission. From Pedro's point of view, there wasn't all that much struggle among the lay people, certainly not to the extent that the elders agonized over it. He didn't know of anybody who quit his game over Hinckley's admonishments. Poker was the real religion for these players and they often observed the Sabbath as many as three times a week, tithing regularly, taking their odd communion in the form of chain-restaurant pasta.

The night I got buzzed in, there were about eight regulars, most starting modestly with racks of about $300. They were an unswerving bunch, adhering to long-entrenched styles of play. An IT manager, for example, never entered a pot with any starter weaker than ace-king. A Greek-restaurant owner, out of superstition perhaps, hammered any hand with a five in it. The play was quick, predictable, and quiet, with as much attention being paid to a rebroadcast of a WPT event as the game itself. "A Moby-Dick?" asked one player after "play-by-play" man Vince Patten named an ace-queen starting hand. "What the hell is that?"

"A monster," said one of the players. Aahs of recognition went around the table, although the IT manager wondered why anyone would risk a chip on that sketchy a hand.

Missing, unfortunately, was Alexi, a wild Russian who dresses flamboyantly ("He has Adidas jumpsuits in every possible color," I was told), bets heavily (Alexi alone is permitted buy-ins over the $500 limit), and plays so badly that phones ring out through all of Salt Lake City as soon as he shows up. However, on this night, the quiet and practiced play of the regulars was enlivened by Shotke, a semi-regular, who rolled into the game with two golf buddies. Shotke was a character, to the extent he wasn't the most obnoxious person you ever met. It's a fine line. He ridiculed everybody's play, characterized current events according to his own personal theology, and was just generally overbearing. The thing was, he was kind of funny. And he bet furiously, amping up the action, goading his two golf partners into spectacular misplays, and drawing everybody else into quickly growing pots.

While I was there, he was lucky as hell. He was amassing huge smokestacks of chips that, comically, seemed to be coming at his partners' expense. One of them didn't seem all that familiar with the game, was one problem. He fervently believed in the power of the flop, whereby an unsuited five-two would surely become an inside straight. It never did. Yet he kept buying back in, to the approximate tune of $1,300 during my stay. He wasn't getting any luckier, certainly no smarter.

Some of the regulars cashed out by ten p.m. but other regulars were just arriving at midnight. As for me, with nothing to gain or lose, I found the game was losing its fascination, and I bailed by one a.m.

I roused Pedro from bed the next day with a two p.m. phone call. He told me the night got predictably crazy as soon as I left, that he had to open a second table, and that he didn't get home until seven a.m. I wanted to know, specifically, how Shotke had done. First, he said, I should know that the idiot golf buddy had somehow rallied to get ahead by several thousand. Second, in a memorable showdown, Shotke engaged him in a $3,000 pot and gutted him. Finally, Shotke, the beer machine probably not helping his play at five a.m., dumped everything, as predicted. Pedro said, furthermore, that Shotke, fatally frustrated, gathered his pals, got on a seven a.m. flight to Las Vegas, and was, last he had heard, playing baccarat at Caesars Palace.

All in all, said Pedro, it had been a wonderful evening. And in less than five hours, he'd be reopening the room for the Thursday-night game, religion be damned. He heard Alexi might show up and he'd put all his regulars on high alert.

Grand Champions, Dead Game Losers, and Fur on Fire

Say you're hiking through some grassy fields in the South Carolina low country and you come across a plot of land studded with blue plastic barrels, all lying on their side, straw spilling out. Closer inspection, if you're the curious sort, shows lengths of eight-hundred-pound-test chains outside them, the heavy links tethered to rusted truck axles. The ground around them is scratched bare. Nearby trees have some sort of bait hanging from the low branches. Old belts—from a treadmill?—are scattered about. Odd scene. At this point, you might be inclined to come closer, puzzle this out, see what's in those barrels.

Don't.

What you've stumbled upon—and so far you haven't stumbled into a trip wire and been blasted with birdshot—is a small pit-bull plantation, a championship nursery, a training camp for some of the finest fighting dogs in the country. This would be a good place to trace a retreat, not so much because the dogs represent a threat (they're on a three-foot "leash," most likely), but because you've just accidentally penetrated one of the most secretive, violent, and moneyed subcultures in America. Yeah, you should probably hike back where you came from. I would go a little faster than that, if I were you.

Whether it's our children's education or our employees' 401(k)s, there is hardly anything we won't bet on. That much we know. It's no longer possible to be shocked by our eagerness to subject every imaginable turn of events to a recreational whimsy. When I read that bettors in India had pooled $33 million after a preschooler had fallen into a well, I admit to having been a little disturbed but not very surprised. It was a grisly proposition but not so much unlike our own insurance industry. We make those kinds of bets all the time. In any case—I'm obliged to report—the little guy survived and the optimists got paid. But there has to be a line we don't cross, a bet we can't make. Doesn't there?

Take this little operation you've just stumbled upon, where, for the sake of a friendly wager, a supposedly lower life-form is sacrificed for the entertainment of a supposedly higher one. If there really is a line, we could be standing on it.

But this is so far underground, you simply don't hear much about it. The Humane Society of the United States tries to keep track of this culture but hardly knows whether to be encouraged or to despair when it comes to its rightful elimination. John Goodwin, who is in charge of animal-fighting issues for the HSUS, told me that while attitudes have changed toward such obvious cruelty among so-called "dog men," the demographic seems to be shifting to a much crueler cult. It's becoming the sport of urban gangsters, who do not even observe the competitive glory of the dogs they end up destroying. "Just another rapper caught up in blood rapture," he once said of the hip-hop artist Jay-Z, who included a scene of dog-fighting in his "99 Problems" video.

Goodwin told me that every so often, local authorities do came upon an operation like the one he described for me above (although, once, it was a surveyor; he really did set off a trip wire—he lived), and there's a brief newspaper account: fifty-nine pit bulls seized, a couple treadmills taken, high-end veterinary equipment, including IVs and medicines like Azium. Less high-end veterinary equipment: A stapler.

Somewhat less frequently, they infiltrate a contract match, where dogs, which in this strange blood sport are as famous as Mike Tyson was in his, are faced off according to Cajun Rules.

It might be a three-card show, with just the owners and necessary "officials" on hand. Perhaps $100,000 is at stake, plus side bets, not to mention the money-making reputation it ensures. A champion (a dog that has won three times) or a grand champion (a dog that's won five times without a loss—abbreviated GC in the puppy personals) commands tremendous breeding fees. A pit bull pup that can be traced to Yellow, the legendary Redboy/Jocko, the Secretariat of dog-fighting, for example, goes for thousands of dollars.

Or, less likely, it could be a genuine spectator sport, with forty people inside a barn, betting Rowdy against Lil' Hitler (these names have *not* been changed). The anticipation of one recent match was so great—and the need for secrecy correspondingly intense—that dozens of participants were directed to a Texas Wal-Mart parking lot, relieved of all cell phones, and led on a three-state caravan that ended up in Mississippi. Before dog-fighting was a felony in forty-eight states, the practice was somewhat more brazen. An agent for the Humane Society of the United States went undercover several decades ago and managed to attend a fight in Arkansas—more like a county fair than an underground dog fight; there were 250 people paying $35 a head, buying barbecue and drinks inside the barn—and eventually participated in the confiscation of $500,000. But dog people, grown necessarily secretive, agree that such attention-getting fanfare is just stupid, this day and age.

Whatever little the authorities do discover, they're quite sure it's hardly representative of the dog-fighting scene. Goodman told me there may be as many as thirty thousand people involved, carefully breeding select strains for "gameness," "wind," or "hard mouth," training these dogs in lap pools, making them hang by their jaws from fly poles, running them on treadmills in two-month training periods before a contract match. And, he said, there is big money on the line. "Big-time drug dollars are in it now," he said. "For them, the fun is in the gambling. They can make tons with a winning dog."

Accordingly, they are incredibly clandestine, even clever. Although there is no disguising the intended career for a pup sold over the Internet—not when its pedigree is traced to a dog like the legendary 8XW Firecracker—the players are too smart to tip anybody to actual matches. Very occasionally there might be an account of a fight in online journals— "Bozo has opened up the black's front leg and the black is weakening" is one I discovered on the Internet—but it is slyly marked "fiction." If there is more explicit journalism out there, you can't see it. The *Sporting Dog Journal,* which was long the *Ring* magazine of dog-fighting until the publisher was himself convicted on dog-fighting charges, was only available by referral until it closed shop.

To realize that there are still this many people wagering on dog fights, coast-to-coast, in big cities as well as rural hamlets, is something of a shock. It does not speak particularly well to a growing awareness of animal rights, for one thing. Nor is it a very impressive recommendation for the human condition—in this day and age. It's true, we all have a lot to answer for when it comes to the treatment of our animals. I trained my golden retriever to dance on his hind legs for a piece of cheese. I suppose this was entirely for my own amusement, as I never caught him doing it on his own. For that matter, it's possible he was even less inclined to dance on his hind legs than a pit bull is to fight (until dogs are as tightly bred to tango as pit bulls are to bite each other in the hindquarters, this is probably true). So maybe we're all in this together.

But although I was just as much a god to my dog as so-called dog men are to theirs (I even ordained the exact time of his death, as any responsible owner would), I have to believe I was simply a mischievous god, not a bloodthirsty one. I did not otherwise participate in his doom, organizing his DNA through rigorous inbreeding until he was a helpless killing machine, so conditioned for combat that his now-exaggerated tenacity could only lead him to his own destruction.

In any case, Willie, for all his potential resentment over our parlor tricks, was never reduced to a smear of blood and snot for the sake of a bet. I got a few laughs out of him, but not a livelihood, and certainly not a dubious simulation of manhood, as one might get through extra-species proxy when it comes to fighting.

But the persistence of this blood sport is daunting. The dog men, who seem to believe they're celebrating an animal's "gameness," just get driven a little further underground, although usually obliging authorities are finding the practice less and less romantic, to judge by the prosecution lately. Goodwin believes there may be one thousand of the old-time sportsmen left, players who call themselves the "core." "But they're in decline," he said, hurt by prosecution, that varies widely throughout the United States. Sentencing in South Carolina, for example, is vigorous. The guy who set the booby traps there, David Tant, got four years. Other figureheads in the sport, Goodwin said, will no longer "get in the box in the U.S." A breeder he calls the "Tony Soprano of the dog-fighting world" only makes appearances in Mexico.

Harder to prosecute, though, is the urban dog-fighting scene. A new breed of handlers has incorporated this rural pastime into their own thug life, enacting their version of hip-hop macho in alley throwdowns (you can catch glimpses of dog-fighting in occasional rap videos, references in lyrics). Accordingly, and quite surprisingly, New York City has more dog-fighting these days than old hotbeds like South Carolina or Louisiana. In Chicago, a longtime cop turned anti-cruelty investigator, told me the gangs do not operate by Cajun Rules, or any rules, for that matter. "It's all about money, pride," he said. "And when the dogs don't deliver, they're gone." Losers get duct-taped to the railroad. "They don't draw scratch lines, if that's what you're getting at."

But wherever it happens, it's not pretty. Although dogs do not necessarily fight to the death anymore ("dead game losers" tend to die of their injuries after the fact), it is still enough of a flesh-torn affair—blood and tissue everywhere—that there is simply no disguising the cruelty, no excusing the pleasure, no justification by zoological imperative. This is what animals are obliged to do? Really? Or is this just what man is capable of doing?

In late 2005, Cook County police ran a four a.m. raid in rural Illinois and broke up a match attended by at least thirty people, some having come from as far away as Alabama. The account that followed noted that T-shirts were being sold, and that one of the spectators, who didn't succeed in fleeing into nearby cornfields, was caught jamming money into his pockets. Thousands of dollars were said to be on the line. The cops found the usual stuff—a pit with two-foot-high walls, the washtub where dogs are scrubbed before the match to prevent any chemical chicanery, scales, medical equipment. Steroids. The usual. Also a dog—who knows his pedigree now, whether he sprang from the Chinaman bloodline or even whether he was a 3XC himself, or maybe so finely bred and trained for bite that he had become a GC and been the point of this whole affair—his carcass now smoldering in a fire the "dog men" had set to destroy the evidence, but didn't quite.

Cape Vincent, New York

Mortal Locks, $30,000 Packages, and Three Squares a Day

The wind blows pretty cold and pretty strong off Lake Ontario, sweeping over snow-covered dairy land, relentlessly pushing at barn sides so that most of the wooden structures you see are in drunken tilts, reclining winter-by-winter. Not that an upright barn would be a particularly comfortable place to be. If you were to live here in this part of upstate New York—and not many do—you would have had to make peace with a more or less constant draft. The wind gets through boards, inside windows, and up your trouser cuffs. The wonder is that the farm buildings don't give up much sooner than they do.

The people that do live here pretend not to mind, in the self-conscious assimilation of hometown pride. "I love the cold," a prison counselor told me, explaining he moved north from Brooklyn just so he could enjoy more of it. And he had just received plenty; it was only a few days after a cold snap that sent temperatures plunging to −21°F and, though surprisingly sunny in the storm's aftermath, it was still snot-cracking frigid. A guard, giving me the kind of disclaimer you always hear when it comes to indefensible life choices, explained the advantage of such a freeze: "It's good for the ice fishing."

The prison, though, seemed airtight. Built in 1988 as part of a prison-building boom in New York State, the Cape Vincent Correctional Facility, originally dubbed Air Rikers for its ability to handle the overload from down South, was definitely made to withstand the kind of blasts that scour the Thousand Island region every winter. Maybe it was more a matter of keeping people in than the wind out, but there was definitely a hermetic feel to it. There were three strands of razor wire encircling the concrete plant. "This is medium security," said my cold-loving counselor. "Maximum security, that's four strands."

Within all this wire-and-concrete block, and past five different iron-clanging checkpoints, resided a former bus salesman, a one-time football star who had gone on to lead a peaceful, if mostly unremarkable life in Dayton, Ohio. Nearing sixty, Doug Warner looked about as fit—and, at six-four, certainly as tall—as he did playing tight end for the University of Cincinnati forty years before. A shaved head gave him a military look, policelike even; if you lined him up with the eight Suffolk County officers it took to take him down and get him in cuffs, you'd be hard pressed to identify the guy who traveled thirteen hundred miles by car with a travel bag containing duct tape, a stun gun, a pistol, and a bulletproof vest, determined to get his money back from what he believed was the mob. He looked that ordinary.

But he was ordinary, is ordinary. It's true, there's this gap of about two years when he was quite desperate and capable of astonishing behavior. But he lays that off on a midlife crisis, a depression that was further complicated by the loss of his job and a volatile stock market that was endangering his retirement savings. That might be an easy way out—the prison counselor who was with me when I visited Warner pretended to doze when he heard Warner's rationalization—but just how else do you square the behavior of a man who on his first visit to Las Vegas refused to put so much as a quarter in a slot machine (his ex-wife testified to the court that he spent most of their vacation there looking for a place to work out) with that of the guy who was caught trying to smuggle $52,000 in cash past airport security on one of his next trips there?

For all my traveling across our coast-to-coast casino, visiting every nook and cranny of this vast bingo hall, Cape Vincent was the single most chilling stop, and not just in the rather obvious meteorological sense. I had hoped, on my rambles, to demonstrate the absolute inevitability of gambling, half-assuming that its commonplace—long underground, now not so much—would make the case for acceptance and understanding. I wasn't about to suggest it was entirely benign; there is plenty about gambling to beware—some of it, I would suggest, to outright outlaw. But mostly, I felt (and mostly still do), gambling is here to stay, an industrialized recreation that we're simply going to have to make our peace with.

But then I met Doug Warner. For all his size, for all his vaguely frightening, bullet-headed appearance, Warner is actually an extremely mild-mannered man, a shock of normalcy in these conditions. He is not much given to adventure, wild ambitions, or grandiose hopes. Although he long harbored a desire to run his own business, he had spent his entire career in sales jobs, working for somebody else. "The next best thing," he told me. He worked for an oil company, an auto parts outfit, had a job in home improvement. For the last eleven years of his career he was earning commissions at Whitworth Bus Sales, enjoying ever larger paydays as his territory grew, putting vans, school buses, transit vehicles into service throughout Ohio.

He was, in other words, like everybody you've ever met. He might have been, for that matter, just like you. Except, of course, he was in prison. For Doug Warner, gambling was not fun, never was, never would be. Gambling was an opportunistic virus, which easily overcame his immune system, no matter his religious or political inoculations, and transformed this simple host into another, scary and unrecognizable figure.

In 2001 Doug Warner was taking home about $80,000 a year, able to bank $50,000 of that, piling up a nice retirement stake in a variety of mutual funds. He was reaching that point in American adulthood, promised but not always delivered, when a comfortable life is finally fulfilled. "You know how they say, life begins when you're fifty, when your kids' college is paid for, you can take better vacations? Well, it's true." If Warner had any regrets over working for somebody else, they were mostly smothered by the rewards of middle-class employment. It wasn't out of the question that he and his longtime live-in would end up somewhere south, Florida maybe, and not that long from now.

But that year "the old man" stepped down as head of his company and was replaced by Kevin Whitworth, and instead of expanding the company and taking it in new directions, the son set upon a policy of contraction, at least as far as Warner was concerned. He told Warner his commissions were being cut from 33 percent to 25 percent and he would have to develop a new territory. He was essentially firing Warner.

Warner took the hint, bailed out, and entertained a few offers but found nothing interesting. There was a job possibility in Washington, DC, but he wasn't making a move that, geographically speaking, was strictly lateral. "Somewhere south," he said, "maybe then." So for 2001 and 2002, he sat around, bought a little Internet company, a retail distributorship, but mainly just puttered around, checking his stock funds on the computer, hoping something would come along.

Those were bad years to be hoping for something to come

along and truly awful years to be watching stock funds on a computer. Even in his retirement accounts, which were conservatively managed, there were wild, sickening swings of fortune. At first up, but then steadily down. Sitting in front of his computer, he watched an IRA go from $90,000 to $80,000 to $70,000. When you are unemployed, in your late fifties, and your assumptions of a comfortable retirement are being daily betrayed by the dot.com implosion, you might begin to entertain ideas that ordinarily wouldn't pass muster in a previous, more certain life. "I thought, you know there's got to be something I can do with my money," he said, "because this, it's going nowhere. It's going down. And then I thought, I know football."

This is a fantastic leap in logic, of course, and probably does say more about the vulnerability of a man who's unemployed and anxious about his future than it does about his capacity for common sense. Because Warner did not particularly know football and, even if he had, he most definitely did not know how to leverage his knowledge to any profit. He had never made a bet in his life, not in Las Vegas, not in an office pool, not on the street. He had not been aware, for example, that it wasn't enough to pick the winner. "There's a point spread," he remembered learning, as if he'd been startled by its existence. "It turns out that's the key to the whole thing." He could hardly have been more naive or less prepared.

And so, he embarked on a strange, tragic journey, during which he would meet shadowy characters, join a mysterious syndicate, travel to Las Vegas on a weekly basis, and make nerve-wracking bets of $20,000 and more. He would argue with his banker when his funds could not be liquidated quickly enough, he would argue with his fiancée—his wife, he calls her—over his spending. He would stand impatiently in secure rooms at the Las Vegas airport while DEA dogs sniffed his money for a possible drug explanation. He would scramble

up and down the Strip, desperate to get money down on
bizarre three-game parlays, the games all fixed, he was assured.
He would lose it all, forfeit his middle-class life and any hope
of a comfortable retirement in winter sunshine, and he would
serve his later years, a day at a time, roaming the halls of Cape
Vincent Correctional Facility, green short-sleeves even in the
winter, collecting garbage in the morning, mopping floors in
the afternoon.

But first he took $2,500 in cash to a Western Union facil-
ity at a local Kmart store and directed it to an offshore casino
in Costa Rica. This was, in itself, a wild flier, but hardly disastrous. Perhaps millions bet online; it can be a fairly harmless
diversion and, if nothing more, accounts for our unseemly
interest in college football games beyond the top twenty,
beyond our own geographical, rooting borders. How did
Arkansas State do, anyway?

Once his account was activated, he began betting college
football, mostly $100 a game, never more than $500. "I did a
very poor job," he said. Still, he felt it would be possible to
earn a return on his investment—not gambling, he pointed
out, investing—and ended up plumping his offshore account
to $10,000, at which point Western Union refused to wire
any more of his cash out of the country.

If a five-figure sum was enough to trigger currency safe-
guards at a local Kmart, it was certainly enough to raise interest on the other end as well. Warner started getting phone
calls from betting services—he had included his number with
his offshore casino setup—that encouraged him not to give
up. And this was just when he was ready to give up. "This was
nuts," he said, "this is the same thing everybody else is doing.
I was disgusted and would have let go, except for the phone
call."

The caller told him, of course he was losing, he didn't

have any information. How could he hope to win, to overcome the line, to overcome the commission, without information? The caller, a man named Blackie, explained that he was in the information business and that Warner could have some of that information if he was willing to pay 25 percent on the back end. This seemed almost fair to him; Warner paid nothing for losers and a rightful quarter for winners. How Blackie could keep track of what was owed—Warner, after all, would be betting with a separate entity—was a mystery to Warner. The honor system, he guessed. Although, somewhat mysteriously, Blackie did seem to know what and where he was betting and called him on it a couple of times. Warner would get no more picks, unless he came up with the 25 percent on his winners.

Well, that wasn't going to be a real problem, as it turned out. Blackie couldn't deliver any winners and Warner managed to go through $25,000 more. Even Blackie recognized this wasn't working and recommended he work with a colleague, a man named Frank. Warner overlooked the fact that Frank would likely be accessing the same information—or noninformation, in this case—as Blackie would have been. But a change in scenery couldn't hurt. Frank worked him up to $5,000 bets—he usually only handled clients capable of betting $10,000 a game, but he'd made an exception for Warner—and delivered him three losers in four weeks. "When you think about this," Warner admitted, "you just have to shake your head." There is no evidence that Warner ever actually paused to think about it, ever shook his head, ever stopped answering the phone.

The next call he got was from a man who called himself Tom Murphy, a personable guy who used more of a soft sell than the touts before him. Murphy easily established a rapport with Warner, a fellow Catholic-grammar-school student, and they exchanged stories of growing up in all-boys schools. Murphy always signed off saying, "Whenever you're tired of losing, talk to me."

Warner was indeed sick of losing. He was sick of looking at his withered retirement account, sick of hearing about it from his incredulous fiancée, sick of wondering about his increasingly bleak future. He called Murphy back, was handed off to another guy, who was quite a bit rougher around the edges, and got a pitch different from all the others—incredible, yes, but so much more persuasive. Lou Dadone explained that his operation, Platinum Sports Advisory, was basically a mob front, a powerful fixer of games, with refs and quarterbacks across the country in its pocket. Dadone said Platinum couldn't quite guarantee every game but that no client had ever lost twice in a row. The way Dadone spelled it out, it was practically to the customer's advantage to take a hit on a game, because then he knew to double, triple, quadruple up on the next game. Dadone told Warner he presently had about eighty people who were going to Las Vegas to exercise his picks and each was putting between $20,000 and $40,000 per game; every week Platinum was forcing $1.6 million, minimum, through the system. "Doug," he said, "we're going to put you on the casino side of the bet."

Dadone said Platinum's specialty was the occasional three-team parlay—all three games would have to cover the spread to win—that paid bettors back sixfold. True odds on such a bet ought to be eight to one, the spread of this novelty wager leaking enormous value out of the proposition, but Warner failed to do the math. One of Las Vegas's biggest sports bettors, a man who constantly does the math, laughed when I told him about the team's specialty. "A three-team parlay is historically a sucker bet," he said. "Sports books beg for that money." Somebody who works in a sports book told me, "The reason we build sports books is because of parlays. The hold in a sports book is only 3 to 4 percent. If you look at parlay cards, the hold goes between 28 to 35. We'll pick these guys up in a limo."

But Warner was impressed with the idea of six to one; he could get well quickly with multiples like that. Warner told Dadone it sounded good but he was down $25,000 and probably couldn't afford to hang with Dadone's crowd. Dadone said, tell you what, you got, say, $5,000 in an offshore account? Here's three teams, see what happens. "The next day," Warner said, "I had thirty grand in my account."

Warner now understands the beauty of the ploy. Had he lost, Dadone would have simply written him off and moved on to the next mark, nothing ventured on his side. But if the bet came through, as it was bound to from time to time, it would take a lot of subsequent disappointment to put Warner in anything like a state of suspicion. He would remember the thrill of a six-to-one payday for a long time.

But he'd have to pay to play. Platinum wasn't like the other services Warner had worked with. At Platinum, the bettor had to put the money upfront to be privy to that week's can't-miss. And at Platinum this was a bit different from the TV touts that promised mortal locks for a $9 phone call. The schedule at Platinum required the customer to buy a $30,000 package that would buy him $120,000 worth of winnings. When the bettor reached that level, he'd need to re-up with Platinum to get the whole thing going again. That was just for the routine weekly cinch, though. The three-team parlay, which only came along several times a season, would cost him $80,000—half upfront. But Warner would be making $350,000 to $500,000 on those bets, all sure things. Platinum owned those games.

Warner said Dadone instructed him to mail him the cash—no checks, of course. Warner by then didn't question that. When he'd originally asked a contact at Platinum for a brochure, a pamphlet, anything in writing, he was nearly laughed off the phone. Do you think the mob puts out pamphlets, he was told. Just put the cash, the first $70,000—$30,000 for the $120,000 package and $40,000 for the first payment in the parlay—in the overnight mail, come out to Las Vegas to meet the gang, and prepare to get rich.

Warner did as he was told, flew to Las Vegas, which took some doing coming from Dayton, and met everybody at the Mirage, where a room had been prepared for him. The initial meeting actually took place at the pool, where Dadone and George Villano—a Platinum hireling, Warner assumed—sized him up. "They wanted to make sure I wasn't wired," Warner said. There were three other men there, identified as nephews, as well as two 350-pound bodyguards. Dadone was flashing a roll of hundreds, paying for drinks. Warner was impressed, although he might not have been in such awe if he'd remembered that those hundreds had only recently been mailed from his home in Dayton.

Later the gang gathered at the Mirage's Baccarat Bar, a small piano lounge. Warner looked around and realized the bar had been closed off for them. The bodyguards stood at the entrances to maintain their privacy. Warner was fully satisfied with their bona fides by now; this was the mob all right. Dadone gave him a game to bet that weekend and he won $10,000. Next trip, he was told, bring the $40,000, the second payment for the three-team parlay bonanza that was coming up Thanksgiving. Meantime, there'd be a game, or a teaser (another sports-book sucker bet) for him every week.

Warner came out every week that season in 2003, and it essentially became a full-time job. He'd make arrangements to leave Dayton every Thursday—he had to be in Las Vegas Friday to get his pick—and would suffer the usual insults of the airline industry, connecting in Minneapolis, Charlotte, and even New York. He'd sleep in airports, in buses, wherever. After his first two visits, he was no longer being put up at the

Mirage, either. And the airport limo wasn't meeting him as promised, for which Dadone kept apologizing. For that matter, he never saw the Platinum gang again. "They led me to believe they were meeting with the others," Warner said.

Warner was on his own, arriving in Las Vegas and taking an $8 bus trip—"I wasn't going to spend $40 on a limo"—to whatever hotel had a good Internet rate. He stayed at the Mirage and the even-pricier Bellagio at first, but thereafter mostly at the Flamingo for $40 a night. For all his duffels of cash, he was no high roller. "I wasn't there to be wined and dined," he said. "I was there to do something with my money, to get out of this hole, to get my wife off my back."

And then each Friday or Saturday morning he'd get the call and he'd have to scramble up and down the Strip to get his money down. Most sports books have limits, although Warner discovered the Mirage would take almost anything. Dadone told him that when it came time to bet the three-team special, a fleet of runners would have to be deployed to get all their game-breaking money down. Meanwhile, though, it was a lot of work to make these bets and it wasn't making him rich. He was winning his share but he was nowhere close to attacking the tremendous fee structure Platinum had imposed. He was doing better in an offshore account, unbeknown to Platinum, where he had built up winnings of $100,000. Even so, he was by no means close to square.

Nor, if Platinum had its way, would he ever be. Over the course of the season, Warner had confided that he wasn't in this so much to get rich as to simply recoup his losses and regain a handle on his retirement. Dadone said he understood and, come to think of it, might have something Warner would be interested in. A lot of the boys were dabbling in the development of offshore Internet casinos themselves. The casinos usually started slow but gradually ramped up to the point where they would provide a steady income stream. One of the nephews separately mentioned that Lou had put him in just such a vehicle and it was now, finally, going great guns. Dadone, as it turned out, had another opportunity pretty much like that. It required an upfront investment of $120,000— cash, of course—but the 10-percent stake ought to return about $30,000 a year, the oddly specific, strangely relevant amount that Warner had been able to live on back in Dayton. Had Warner happened to mention that?

Warner said he was in. Funding his investment was problematic, though, because Dadone always wanted to be paid first. Warner couldn't understand why he couldn't just let his winnings run and pay for his share of the company down the line, a lump sum. Dadone would have none of that and insisted every $10,000 payday, whenever it came, go toward the business, leaving Warner to scrounge for his gambling stake anew every week.

Well, there was always the three-teamer coming up on Thanksgiving, that certain special situation that got everybody right, no matter how his luck had been running. Warner had been getting antsy, skeptical even, and was beginning to tape their calls. Still, when he got the call for the three-teamer, he broke down the last of his mutual funds—the $52,000 that represented his remaining retirement account—and flew back into Las Vegas. A six-to-one payday would put him exactly even. He needed this.

Dadone and his crew met Warner at the Mirage, expecting he'd arrive with his usual $10,000. They were bug-eyed when they realized how much he'd actually brought. They said they needed $46,000 of that, off the top, for the business. The business! It was as if they couldn't bear to see Warner with so much uncommitted cash. Warner might have argued that the money was to be bet, to be pyramided into a gigantic and well-earned windfall, out of which any investments could then, and only then, be made. "But I don't know what came over me," Warner said. "I just let 'em do it. I'm not a confrontational person and they just kind of led me, and I just followed."

The Platinum crew told him to take the remaining money and bet it on the parlay, and, if he was smart, to use up what he had left in his offshore account to get in on the same action. Warner felt that his offshore account was particularly irritating to Platinum; it was money they simply could not get at. Warner put everything he had left into play, went back to his room to watch a bit, down to the gym to work out. He admitted that he didn't always watch the games. He'd check in afterward, see how he'd done, but mostly avoided as much of the Las Vegas experience as possible, even to the point where he seldom bothered to watch his savings at work.

Which were now gone. The parlay that required the compounding of three distinct miracles did not come through. He had lost more than $70,000 and was looking at a penniless future. He called his contact at Platinum, back in Long Island, New York, and wondered what had just happened to him. George Villano acted equally stunned. "We're checking on it," he said. "Lou's on it right now, in fact, he's out of town. Just get cleaned up, get out of town, go home and we'll get back to you by Tuesday." Villano did let him know that another three-teamer situation, the kind that you wait once a season for, was coming up again in a couple of weeks. He might think about some makeup bets.

Warner was furious, with Platinum, with himself. "I knew I'd been had," he said. But he was also absurdly desperate. There was absolutely no way he, out of work and now fifty-eight, could ever make back his retirement account. The only way, really, was to somehow hit a three-teamer, or one of Platinum's teasers. "Now the only way I have to get a substantial amount of money is to gamble." He borrowed $20,000 of his wife's savings, flew back to Las Vegas, got his orders, and, placing it in a variety of teasers and parlays, cashed out with $70,000. "And now," he said, "I'm back in the game."

Platinum thought they'd seen the last of Doug Warner but, after he'd repaid his wife her $20,000, he was still newly flush with $50,000, $30,000 of which he had dedicated to betting. Which, over the next four weeks, he lost. After he'd lost the final $5,000 (he had $20,000 at home, which he'd for once decided was untouchable), he discovered that Platinum's phone had been disconnected. He had paid Platinum $225,000 for services and 10 percent of a business and he had lost $75,000 in actual gambling. His life savings. And now he really was done. "I was through."

Touts have been around as long as there have been games to bet. The promise of inside information, with presumably verifiable results ("We crushed Las Vegas on last week's Game of the Century"), has made them an attractive option to guesswork for the unsophisticated bettor. But, in fact, they belong more to the telemarketing industry than they do to the gambling business. Their success depends entirely on their pitch, quite a bit less on their ability to deliver the game of the century, year, or week.

Consider this: Of the thirty handicappers who are presumably both honest and confident enough to submit to independent monitoring (as tabulated by Sports Watch), eighteen were losers for their clients over the 2004 NFL season. Want to get well during March Madness? Of the fifteen who paid Sports Watch to keep track, for the sake of advertised documentation (remember, these were the good guys!), eleven were losers. Of course, some did win, but not consistently enough to recommend a particular methodology. The top NFL handicapper from 2003, Triple Threat, won an impressive 60 percent of its picks (the spread included). In 2004, it was second to last, with only 42 percent winners. It's as if it were a matter of luck, almost.

And these are the guys who practice aboveboard. For the most part, the industry is the last refuge of con artists, fast-talking pitchmen reading boilerplate scripts, practicing a sell so hard it could cut glass. That initial $9 call can get turned into a $1,000 package in about the time it takes to read your credit card number into the phone. One tout, arrested in a Fort Myers, Florida, operation, admitted what ought to be obvious: "No one knows anything," said Robert Robitzek, who used three aliases while working for National Sports Consultants. "If we had any kind of information, why would we need any customers." Robitzek, who later bought the business and named it Players Edge, insisted it was "an ugly business, but legal." He said, "We don't have information on the games, we don't have referees and we don't have players and coaches." Just the ability to work seventy hours a week, making four to five hundred phone calls, massaging their losers. For his effort, the government discovered, Robitzek made $761,134 in three years.

And when you lose, which you are bound to, your name gets passed along to another "company," which means the guy working in another cubicle, with presumably better, if pricier information. I was told of one outfit in Las Vegas that's home to ten different "companies," each willing to sell a package of mortal locks, based on player injuries, team trends, or the coach's biorhythms, for as long as your money holds out.

Incredibly there are not many complaints. In Las Vegas, where handicappers post bonds and fill out questionnaires to become registered, the commissioner of consumer affairs told me there hadn't been a beef in the ten years she'd been there. "I don't know why," she said, laughing. It's apparently been consigned to that area of silly science, like astrology, where you get what you deserve. Would you complain if your fortune cookie lied? Or would you be too embarrassed to admit you took it seriously?

Every once in a while, a consumer affairs department will look into it, but you don't often hear of crackdowns. The kind of person who would dedicate ten grand to the belief that somebody in a strip-mall office has two hundred team trainers on his Rolodex is not what you'd call a sympathetic victim. It's difficult to get somebody to battle on your behalf when you just paid $500 for a Championship Plus package that was most likely some flimflam man reading the Gold Sheet back to you. It's every man for himself in this jungle.

Still, this is neither the country nor the age where anybody deserves to be held personally responsible for flagrant foolishness, not as long as there's someone else willing to take on litigation. Occasionally, very occasionally, the insult to pride and pocketbook is sufficient to provoke an attempt at recompense. One such case, during the course of its legal machinations, uncovered the true workings of this industry, "scamdicappers," as the feds called them.

In the spring of 2003, a millionaire named Tim Bronkhurst got hooked up with National Sports Consultants and Players Edge, who promised him 70 percent success—a doubling or even tripling of his money—in baseball and NBA and college basketball. He had sold his business in 1998 but, in the spring of 2003, was watching his investments flounder during a bad stretch of the market when he heard a radio ad for an 800-number on a San Diego sports-talk show. "We are not looking for gamblers," the infomercial said, "we are looking for investors." When Bronkhurst responded, a man who called himself Frank Russo managed to get the following facts from him: He had never bet on sports, he was worth in the "seven digits," and he was looking for a "genuine business opportunity."

The following is from court documents: Bronkhurst was quickly handed over to the firm's owner, Dan "the Man" Wilson (real name John Rodney), who said he had twenty-five years experience producing near-perfect picks. Wilson said he was necessarily discriminating about his clients and would have to consider Bronkhurst's application. He told Bronkhurst he'd call him within a week to let him know if he was "accepted."

Bronkhurst must have passed muster, because the touts got back to him with the opportunity to get in on their score for an initial fee of $50,000. The same amount would additionally be deposited in a West Antilles booking outfit called Legalbook Sports Fair Deal, just to get him started. Thus began an eighty-one day orgy of gambling, during which Bronkhurst paid a total of $1,940,000 to the touts for "advice" and during which he bet $694,804, mostly on basketball. Bronkhurst had what you might call unlimited confidence, at least at first, in the services. During one two-day spell he wired $900,000 to the touts for a baseball package, followed up with a $290,000 check sent to them in overnight mail, and made another wire transfer of $300,000 to Legalbook Sports.

He did not do well. Twice he bet on eight-game NBA parlays, a dozen times he played two-game baseball parlays. He lost twenty-four consecutive parlays and, in fact, never won a single such proposition. In one memorable two-day stretch he was put onto twenty-seven surefire winners; he lost every one of them. He did not, in fact, achieve anything close to 70 percent success. Of seventy-six bets, he won only twenty.

Bronkhurst had fallen in with a bad bunch all right, but not a bunch so bad they could actually fix games. Like Warner, he had been convinced of their ability to not just anticipate outcomes but to direct them. When undercover agents, investigating another complaint from a man who lost $95,000, called the same service, a man who identified himself as Gino DeCarlo told them, "When you're paying guys to throw a game, when you're paying officials to make bad calls, you know it costs a lot of money." It was part of their pitch: This is how you have to do business when you want big returns. Even so, the math didn't really work. If Bronkhurst had won every bet—100 percent—he would have recovered barely a third of his "investment." By the time Bronkhurst was able to recognize the scam, he had disgorged $2.4 million.

Bronkhurst was apparently better at selecting legal help than he was at betting advice. His attorney, using information that the services had made kickbacks to sports books offshore, filed his case under the RICO act, a scary maneuver that puts triple damages in play. The touts chose not to take this particular gamble and, in the interest of making Bronkhurst go away, settled with him for $1 million. Cases like this can go on for three years; this one lasted less than two months. It's not like they didn't have the money (John Rodney made nearly $3 million in less than four years of operation).

In the end, though, the case did not go away and the touts fell when the feds proved kickbacks from the offshore casinos. Citing an operation that "would and did obtain . . . in excess of $22 million to which they were not otherwise entitled," the government came down as hard as it could. It arrested Rodney and thirteen others (only Rodney did jail time) and seized $8 million. Included in the forfeitures was Rodney's house in Estero, Florida, a 2004 Mercedes S430, nearly $1.4 million in three investment accounts, and a rather odd 201-piece inventory of sports memorabilia. The government now has, somewhere, a Joe Montana jersey and a John Elway helmet.

Doug Warner had not lost $2.4 million but it was hardly any comfort to him. If anything, he was actually in far worse straits than Bronkhurst ever was; Warner, unlike Bronkhurst, had lost all he had. Back in Dayton, out of action, he sat and stewed. He contacted a lawyer who explained, that without a paper trail he had no recourse. He sat and stewed some more. He had been weak in his dealings with Platinum, led willy-nilly, just giving up bags of money when asked. But now, removed in time and distance, he was gathering resolve. "Nobody in their right mind," he told me, "regardless of the lies, the deceit, the charade, could allow this to go on. It could not be allowed to go on."

The problem gambler, the person who bottoms out in a shallow pool of desperation, may not be as common as once thought. The figure of 10 percent, which gambling opponents have bandied about, has long been considered that portion of the public that will eventually require help. But at Harvard's division on addiction, they are putting the number closer to 2 percent, tops—about the same as those afflicted with schizophrenia and way less than the 10 percent that fall under alcoholism.

"That's still a robust number," said Christine Reilly, the executive director at the Institute for Research on Pathologic Gambling and Related Disorders, "that's still a lot of people. And for a person destroyed by their gambling problem, the damage is no less real." But she and her colleagues did not seem particularly alarmed (nor blasé, on the other hand) by the growing accessibility of gambling, or even the extent to which society is willing to tolerate it. These are people with addictive problems that just happen to be expressed at the slot machine or in a sports book. "Most of these people have another problem," she told me, "depression, substance abuse, bipolar disorder. We're not always sure what comes first. Of course, losing would certainly depress you, but rarely is gambling addiction a stand-alone disorder."

There is almost certainly a genetic component whereby

people cannot experience the satisfaction of reward normally and must reach for higher stakes to gain pleasure. A day at the beach does not quite cross the threshold of happiness for them, and so they must seek greater payoffs for sensations others feel more easily. And there is, without doubt, a neuro-chemical element. Reilly told me the brain's pathways that get lit up in anticipation of a monetary win are the same as those fired when a cocaine user prepares for a hit.

To me, this seemed frightening news, latent vulnerabilities just waiting for the right casino ad, easy freeway access, or the promise of, say, inside information. Or a state lottery. Or racinos. Or . . . And yet only 1 or 2 percent, according to Harvard's studies, are doomed to disaster because of these hidden software traps, these otherwise worthwhile inclinations toward self-improvement that get twisted and turned under the neon lights. Somehow, amazingly, we mostly adapt to these fine-tuned temptations, even as they continue to surround us. The casinos learn how to ring our bell, all right, but rarely is damage done. Most of us, that 98 percent, set budgets or simply recognize the house edge as the price of fun, or just pass our losses off as so much necessary steam, vented harmlessly, a memorable relief of pressure.

And even when gamblers do go off the edge, there is still the possibility of rescue. Researchers are toying with drugs, the same kind used in alcohol addiction, but also are having success with cognitive behavioral therapy, which might be as fundamental as explaining to the addicted just why the gaming industry trades at such a premium. You really can't win. And, too, there is the human beings' remarkable resiliency. "Most cocaine users get well on their own," Reilly told me. "Most gamblers do, too."

Until they do, of course, there can be some rather spectacular disintegrations of human spirit. Such anecdotes are what galvanizes gambling opponents, far more than the scientific studies can. There is hardly a week that goes by, as far as my clip service can tell, that some member of a religious order has not embezzled church funds to satisfy a gambling debt. I can only assume that these stories make print because of perceived irony. Who knows how many more, less ironic, workers are caught doing the same thing. Not as often, but regularly all the same, there are stories of housewives found brain-fried in front of a video poker machine, their children usually locked in the car in a nearby parking lot. The dopamine, neurotransmitters popping in the expectation of a royal flush, made them do it.

Doug Warner was flat out of dopamine, serotonin—whatever it was that had been triggering episodes of hope, had been modulating his midlife anxiety. Platinum had drained him of all his neurochemical balms and he was back to that previous existence, no longer self-medicated by a wild self-help scheme. He had reached the place where he knew better, understood the house odds, shucked the fantasy of parlays that paid six to one. To an extent, he had gotten well on his own. The thing was, he was also flat out of money.

Warner contacted a private investigator in New York, who secured an address for Platinum Sports Advisory as well as for George Villano, his frequent phone contact. The detective was unable to come up with an address for the far more mysterious Lou Dadone. This was preliminary to Warner's rather simple plan: He was going to New York to get his money back. It shouldn't be hard. He knew, from his conversations with Dadone, that there was always a minimum of twenty-five or thirty grand in the house. Dadone had told him, "You never know when you'll need the money." Warner didn't think that his overnight packages containing $40,000 in cash were going into the bank's Christmas Club. Sure, there'd be cash there.

Warner was in a weird place. Out of money, out of work, his "wife" out of the house because of their disagreements over his gambling. "So I got a gun, my wife's gun, actually," he said, "a bulletproof vest, a stun gun and duct tape." He drove nonstop to New York, took a room at a Holiday Inn on Long Island, and staked out Platinum's offices for three days, noting the comings and goings. On the fourth day, Sunday, he saw Dadone, who, Villano had kept telling him, was out of pocket trying to solve the broken three-teamer, and tried tailing him. Dadone was really the one he wanted to confront, at gunpoint if needed, to force him to return his money. Warner had the feeling it could go wrong—he was still picturing those bodyguards—and recognized the worst-case scenario. "What happens if I find Lou?" he wondered. "Do I shoot him? Does he shoot me? I don't know." Dadone was the mob, after all.

But he lost Dadone in traffic. If his private detective hadn't transposed Dadone's license plate number and had come up with a correct address, he could have proceeded to his home. That opportunity was lost. Warner doubled back to Platinum and renewed his stakeout, this time waiting for Villano to appear. When Villano left for the evening, Warner approached him. Villano was somewhat surprised. "Doug! What are you doing here?"

Warner said Villano full well knew what he was doing here. He wanted his money. Villano was thinking fast. "What are you talking about? Is Lou pulling this shit again? Goddamn Lou! Look, I'm sorry. I've got enough to put that guy in jail myself."

Warner had forgotten for the moment that Villano had been present when Dadone proposed the business investment. If Lou had been "pulling this shit again," it was hardly behind Villano's back. Either way, though, it wasn't solving Warner's problem. "I have a gun," Warner told him, showing him the pistol in his pocket. "Oh, Doug, put that away," Villano pleaded. "We can work this out. We can take care of Lou. He's pulled this crap before, and I've kept him out of trouble. I'll put him in jail if I have to, but let's get this thing settled. Just let me call my wife."

Villano called home and asked how much cash was in the house. His wife evidently told him $4,800, whereupon Villano told her to meet him at the door with the money. He was on his way home, and he was helping a friend out. "And then we'll go on to Disney on Ice," he told her.

This wasn't quite Warner's plan. "This is crazy," he told Villano. "The $4,800 is nothing." Villano explained it was good-faith money, a down payment. "I'll meet you at the office tomorrow morning at ten," he told Warner. "I'll have $100,000 of my money and Lou will make up the difference or else." Or else what, Warner wondered. "Or else he'll go to jail, because I've got enough on him to put him away. He's going to come up with the money."

They drove to Villano's home—Warner had already cased the residence out and had not been pleased to see a Lexus, a Cadillac, a camper, and two Wave Runners in front of a million-dollar home—and got the $4,800. Villano dropped him off at a motel, shook his hand, and told him he'd see him on Monday morning at the office with the cash.

This was not exactly pressing the advantage. But this wasn't the first time that Warner had been convinced of a shaky proposition. Anyway, what else could he do? He returned the next morning but saw no sign of activity or presence. Leaving the gun and the rest of his gear, except for a stun gun and his vest, in a bag in the car, he walked in the door of Platinum, saw nobody, and quickly realized something was not quite right. He turned around and saw eight men in black leather jackets, all hyper, shouting, "Suffolk County sheriffs! Suffolk County sheriffs! Put down the gun! Put down the gun!"

In the context of this rendezvous, their shouts made absolutely no sense to Warner. It had occurred to him that mob goons might be waiting for him, but certainly not the police. "Last thing in the world I expected," he said, "was the mob would go to the police department." A struggle ensued, and ensued, and ensued. Warner was certain they were mob hit men and he resisted mightily, for at least fifteen minutes he thought. If they were cops, he remembered thinking, eight of them surely could have gotten cuffs on him in fifteen minutes. "This is not how cops act, this is not what cops do," he said. "They beat me up pretty good."

When the police finally subdued him, they went on to discover his kidnap kit in the Buick, and they knew they were in business. The district attorney charged Warner with second-degree kidnapping, first-degree robbery, second-degree attempted grand larceny, second- and fourth-degree criminal possession of a weapon, first-degree use of a firearm, unlawful wearing of a body vest, and resisting arrest. It was quite a legal laundry list. If convicted on all charges, Warner faced a maximum of more than one hundred years in prison. His retirement would be assured after all.

From Warner's point of view, his actual crime was paltry. He had shown Villano a gun for twelve seconds (although Villano said he drove home at gunpoint, frightened for his life). And, really, who had gotten hurt? One cop banged his hand on Warner's head, another twisted an ankle. It was more comic than tragic, a Gang that Couldn't Shoot Straight abduction. A guy allows his predator free on the condition he'll return to custody the next morning. And don't forget to bring the $200,000. That's what Warner's plan amounted to, when you boil it down. Yet, once a gun gets put into play, a legal mechanism is shifted into gear and there is no stopping it. Warner could cry all he wanted about the abuses of Platinum but nobody could get past the brandishing of a .38—not the cops, not the DA, not the judge.

Warner was not as relieved as you might expect to get just the two years, even whittled down from a century, in the pretrial. He felt the $20,000 he paid his attorney—exactly the amount that he had decided to bank before his final gambling expedition—earned him the price of a trial, during which Villano and Dadone would surely be exposed for the scoundrels they were. He felt his lifelong innocence—his character—ought to count for something. When he met me at Cape Vincent, he was still carrying around a folder of letters from family and friends, all attesting to his tremendous naïveté. He riffled through them from time to time, as if the testimony were all that assured him of a life prior to this.

I shook Warner's hand on my way out, back into the Upper New York cold, and felt a stab of sympathy for him, for anybody who had to suffer the shock of confinement. It had to be lonely and it had to be exhausting. "The time passes so slow," he told me. "If time passed this slow when you were outside, you could get a lot done." He told me that, in his boredom, he had recently attended his first Gamblers Anonymous meeting. It was a waste, he said, really just something to do. "I'd be shocked," he said, "if somebody told me I had a gambling problem."

On Montauk Highway, between the Ice Palace Idle Hour Gourmet Italian Ices shop and the New Idle Hour Gourmet Deli, is a small storefront, no signage. Inside a thirty-foot rectangular room there are six wooden desks, three against each wall. A lone TV set hangs in the office corner, tuned to a baseball game. There is a threadbare couch along another windowless wall and above it is a four-by-four white board with a list of names. A man who identifies himself as Tom DiAngelo, wearing a blue track suit and smoking a thin cigar, says he's the manager and that neither Villano nor Barba—the man who had been introduced to Warner as Lou Dadone—is presently there (although a white Mercury Mountaineer registered to Elizabeth Barba was parked in a nearby alley). It's still a sports advisory service, he says, though it's no longer named Platinum. He won't say what it's called. As for Warner, DiAngelo says, yeah, he knows the name. "That guy's sick. He came here and tried to kidnap George." Asked why Warner might do that, DiAngelo says, "That guy was smoking crack. He's a gambler and he lost some bets. This is a criminal. He can say what he wants. If you want to believe what a criminal says, that's up to you."

Inside the office, while DiAngelo talks, there are five other men at their desks, sitting under fluorescent lamps. They are working the phones—calling, calling, calling—just in case there is somebody, somewhere in this wonderful country, who wants to double his money, or triple it, or just put all his worries to rest.

Sharks, Marks, and Million-dollar Putts

Golf is another of those recreations that's needlessly dolled up by ritual. It's more than just a good walk spoiled, of course, but it's not quite a sport, either. Or rather, not only a sport. Really—and you can ask any golfer, pro or amateur—it's just one more excuse to wager, to throw cash in the wind. It's a poorly dressed pari-mutuel is what it is. Otherwise, what possible fun could it be? Its advantages of fresh air and wholesome exercise are offset by a bag of tools ill-suited to the task, the enjoyment of the course's pleasant scenery undermined by devilish design (why would you have sand in your yard?), the whole idea of camaraderie compromised by competition. If it weren't for automatic two-down presses, what would be the point in investing so much money in Footjoys?

Anybody who might oppose gambling, on whatever grounds, has to reckon with the simple and overriding fact that gambling makes almost everything more interesting. It makes college basketball interesting, dog-fighting possible, even golf. These activities might be attractive enough on their own, but you have to wonder how passionate you'd feel about Saturday's NCAA action, for example, if you didn't have something riding on it. Gambling is that additive for most of us, the spice in our bland lives. It can goose even the most traditional—dare I say boring?—game in our little pantheon of sports.

Am I getting carried away here? Even the pros, whose interest in a green jacket or Nike endorsement ought to be sufficient to their effort, conduct at least part of their week as if a foursome were simply an ambulating casino. Phil Mickelson, it's been said, plays harder on Tuesdays than on Sundays. Indeed the tour is extremely lively for the exotic wagering that seems to develop out of the workplace environment. Everybody knows about Nassaus, Skins Games, Bingo, Bango,

Bongo. News of $1 million melees, like when Davis Love III, Fred Couples, Justin Leonard, and Tom Kite got involved in a no-bogey contest at Troon in 1997, even leaks out from time to time. But anybody know what an Air Hammer is? Guys on the tour do. It's when a bet gets doubled as soon as the ball leaves the club face. Failure to accept the challenge, which amounts to in-flight razzing, constitutes forfeit. The tour is cutting edge when it comes to golf gambling.

Not that the muni player hasn't been juicing up his game with $5 automatics. Only since the game was invented. The game is so adaptable to betting purposes that it's hard for some golfers to get through a round with even the shirts on their backs. A Harvard study in 2002 found that golf bettors outnumbered the puritans by five to one. And no wonder. Unlike most other games, golf allows the ability to assign handicaps and give the illusion of even-playing fields. It encourages the arrogance of mastery—through swing coaches and outlandishly priced equipment—and also the notion that a superior mind-set trumps all. The inherent unpredictability of a game that depends mightily on the bounce of a ball does not give the golfer, who's just traded in his Big Bertha for the Really Big Bertha after all, sufficient pause when it comes to $100 automatic one-downs. Which is to say, for somebody with a little hustle in his heart, there is a lot to work with.

Anybody who'd try to argue this, insisting on the tradition of an ancient links game, has to deal with another part of golf's history, which is full of some of the most exquisite con artistry known to man. A lot of it is traced to the great Titanic Thompson, who developed an ambidextrous game during its so-called Golden Age in the thirties to cull millions from unsuspecting opponents. Switching stances for the back nine, double or nothing, was his bread and butter. Thompson was a genuinely good golfer—he spotted Byron Nelson three strokes and relieved the great man's backers of $3,000—but he had no ambitions for it as a profession. "I couldn't take a cut in pay," he famously observed, when it was still a gentleman's game. He was far more interested in the edge he could get from golf. His classic ploy: He won $1,000, betting he could drive a ball five hundred yards. Of course, you could, too, if it was on a frozen lake.

For this type of gambler, the golf is almost incidental, just one more forum to operate from. It's more a matter of locating the money and sizing up the competition—wrangling the right handicap—than it is striking the ball. When Bobby Riggs finished up with competitive tennis (but before he began provoking the women's tennis community), he landed at a Florida country club that listed at least 150 millionaires. Riggs, though a relative beginner at golf, couldn't believe his good fortune. So many marks! "It was like an open-air poolroom," he told his biographer.

Gamblers who more typically have to depend on the cut of the card or the throw of the dice revel in a game in which you can, however marginally, actually affect the outcome. To them, the game is found money. And while there are legendary golfers who are gamblers—a young cart man named Lee Trevino cost Thompson $9,000 when Raymond Floyd squeaked by him; and almost all the players on tour today like to heighten the fun with a wager—it seems more likely that the legendary gamblers become golfers.

A lot of them are sharks, the kind of guys who'd challenge you to a game with nothing more in their bags than a baseball bat and a rake. Trevino himself liked to use a Dr Pepper bottle taped to a stick, long before he graduated to the PGA. Trick-shot artists (Thompson practiced chipping balls into shoes for hours until he mastered the "shot") occupy another level of the gambler's caste system. If you honestly believe that the stranger who sidles up to you at the nineteenth hole *can't* hit a four-iron through a partially opened window, then God help you and your rent money.

The real fun is when gamblers get together, to refresh the fluorescent pallor of their faces with the occasional round of golf. They can't help themselves, so grateful to get out from under the crushing probabilities of poker, the NFL, the casino slot magic. Here, finally, is the chance to (metaphorically) load the dice. This is a game they can take apart and, within the confines of a handicap, master to profitable consequence. All they have to do is somehow charm their idiot brethren out of their stake.

The hustles that go on every day, unnoticed by normal citizenry, have passed into gambling legend, that literary limbo where it may or may not have been a $1 million payday, but it doesn't really matter. But there have been some semi-organized affairs—Jack Binion's Golf Gamblers Tournaments or Russ Hamilton's Annual—that really do produce outrageous wagering. They're still talking about Doyle Brunson's thirty-five-footer on the sixteenth hole that won him and fellow poker player Mike Sexton $336,000 in a Binion tourney back in 1998. And that was long after his bum knee—the one that had cost him a basketball career and forced him into a life of poker years before—had completely failed him. According to the reports, there was a fleet of gamblers tagging along in golf carts, the side bets that day producing a frantic flurry of green at every hole.

This kind of activity is probably best left in the gamblers' underworld, but every once in a while the game tries to institutionalize the action for wider consumption. The Skins Game, which is sort of like a progressive slot, where first prize keeps rolling over, was packaged for TV in 1983 and has remained a pretty big success during golf's so-called Silly Season every year since. It's not quite what it was, the sums no longer as amazing as they seemed nearly a quarter-century ago. A $200,000 skin on No. 18 is not as dramatic these days when the average PGA purse is $5 million. And really, does Fred Couples need another quarter-mil?

Another attempt to co-opt the excitement of golf betting was made in 2005, when former NFL quarterback Zeke Bartkowski wondered what would happen if more ordinary golfers—pros, possibly, but of a far less elite stature—competed for a first-place prize of $3 million. On the assumption that that ought to mess with someone's mind, Bartkowski arranged for a four-ball match-play tournament, with (he hoped) 128 teams of two, competing over six days in the wind-blown town of Mesquite, Nevada. The competitors could not come from PGA's major leagues—nobody with exempt status on the big tours, nobody who's been PGA-3 for three years. They'd probably be more gifted than the average hustler, but not so good that you'd recognize a single one of them. In other words, $3 million was going to mean something to them.

Bartkowski only got sixty-four teams to come up with the dough, possibly because the $100,000 entry fee was still steep, no matter how many backers a duffer could get. He decided to keep first prize at the attention-getting $3 million, but pared the others down.

And so, a field of Nationwide Tour players, club pros, and well-heeled amateurs descended on Mesquite, with a considerable wake of professional gamblers toting paper bags full of cash. Russ Hamilton, a World Series of Poker champ who runs his own happy-go-lucky tournament strictly to fleece his friends, showed up to sponsor the best team and then engage the gallery in side bets. He had $100,000 from UltimateBet.com to get started. His duo—John Douma and Mikkel Reese, mini-tour players—typified the field. Good and anonymous.

Out of the same mold were Garth Mulroy and David

Ping, two struggling guys with just enough juice left to scramble to the tee. Ping had yet to get past even the first day of Q School, and was battling mightily on the Nationwide Tour, where his biggest payday had been $10,000 in the IGTA Orlando Classic—two years before. He was—like any golfer—equal parts determined, unlucky, and delusional. "A dime a dozen," he admits.

Ping's story was so typical it ought to be presented as a cautionary tale to every college kid who thinks his swing is the key to the family fortune. Just in the past year he had spent $70,000 to chase down $15,000 in prize money, missing the cut by one or two strokes in fifteen straight tournaments. This is PGA Econ 101; the numbers make sense nowhere else. By the time Bartkowski's tournament—named Big Stakes Match Play—had shown up on his radar, Ping had debts of $140,000 and just $7.53 in the bank. Only thanks to his wife's salary as a first-grade teacher in Whittier, California, could he possibly keep going. Although even he knew he couldn't keep going much longer. "I was at the end of the road," he told me, "and I was thinking about a real job, talking to some friends and relatives about it. It's no fun living broke, trying to chase that dream and getting knocked around. Since that first time I qualified for the Buick in 2001, well, that's coming on five years. Time for a real job."

About all Ping had going for him, in his continued avoidance of a "real job," was a connection. His father was a sports agent and, through him, Ping approached Barry Stokes and Ross Verba, two NFL linemen, who thought it might make for a fun little getaway. And, at just $100,000, cheap.

What he also had going for him was a tolerance for pressure. "Look I made a living, not a big one obviously, making money—not hustling exactly—on the golf course. Two-man best ball? That's about as normal as it gets for me." He was at home with $5 Nassaus, $50 Nassaus even, where you could find yourself chipping for $1,000. It wasn't comfortable, exactly, not on his income. But it was hardly unusual. "I shoot big numbers," he said, "but I can make birdies." This little tournament seemed right up his alley.

Yet Ping was horrified to arrive in Mesquite—which he imagined as his deliverance—and see a field of players, each like him, other guys from the mini-tour, all equally desperate, all with their own connections. This little tournament was up a lot of players' alleys. He was crushed. Maybe he didn't even belong here.

But really, who did? The volatility of the game, its octane rating dialed up by the numbing amounts at stake, would almost certainly disable otherwise healthy egos. Maybe all these guys were pressure players, but there wasn't a one of them who'd ever experienced anything close to this psychological PSI. If the event unfolded properly, there would be some stricken personalities, golfers who once sweated a $100 Nassau, now putting for $3 million, talking in tongues, and bathed in flop sweat. It wasn't going to be fair, but it might be fun to watch.

The UltimateBet team, so highly favored that Hamilton couldn't get any bets down on it, got knocked out the first day by a pair of golfers backed by Michael Jordan. Nobody had gone catatonic, their swing checked permanently at shoulder-height, but it was plain to see that this kind of golf was more like a science experiment than a sporting event. How fragile was the human psyche? We'd see. Jordan's team won its next day's match, too, guaranteeing at least $100,000 and a return on the sponsor's investment, to make the field of sixteen. So it was that sturdy, anyway.

The Ping-Mulroy team was, too; Mulroy acing one hole and firing two eagles and six birdies. "After that," said Ping, "the pressure's off." They at least secured their backers' investment and didn't have to explain to a pair of NFL linemen how a slice on No. 6 cost them the equivalent of an incentive clause or two. Ping and Mulroy began to breathe even easier after Day Four, when they'd guaranteed a total of $400,000. Split four ways, that would help. But after Day Five, a funny thing happened. Everybody got out their Casio calculators, subtracted this and divided that, and decided the second-place prize of $750,000 was chump change. That was only $162,500 apiece? Who could live on that? Ping, who only once in his life had made five figures, admitted it. "You get greedy."

The final day may or may not have been the richest round in golf, but for the four players remaining it was a once-in-a-lifetime opportunity, the kind of chance that might not come their way ever again. "The pressure was surreal in one way," said Ping, "yet when you're on the course you're not actually thinking of the money. You're just wanting to win."

Ping and Mulroy chased down a pair of East Coast country club pros, Mark Mielke and Rick Hartmann, on that final day, nobody giving an inch, nobody bowing to the pressure, nobody paralyzed, reduced to gibberish. Ping chipped brilliantly, giving them a lead at the sixteenth that was never closed. It was a payday of $725,000 each, for the two golfers and their two sponsors, and everybody's career clock got reset.

When I caught up with Ping some months later, he wasn't so much wallowing in his dough as he was enjoying the second chance it gave him. He and his wife were still living in a seven-hundred-square-foot apartment, she was still teaching first grade, he was still hustling at La Habra Heights Golf Club. They had bought two cars, but that was their only concession to sudden wealth. What he was mainly doing was planning another assault on the mini-tour, still hoping for a PGA card down the road.

"In December," he told me, "I've got the Nevada Open." He ticked off a number of events he figured on entering, this

time without having to max out his credit cards. He said golf
was a funny game and you never knew when some mini-tour
player would suddenly explode onto the PGA. "There's no
timeline in golf," he said. "You hear of guys getting their card
at thirty-five all the time." It could happen. The main thing,
he said, was he didn't have to look for that "real job" after all.
"The golfer's nightmare," he said, laughing.

He also told me he planned another try at the Big Stakes
event the next year, although he was discouraged by the news
that Bartkowski had announced first-place money had been
reduced by a full million, the better to reward lower finishes.
"Can you believe it?" Ping asked, laughing again. "Two million?" Minus the entry fee, split four ways—what was left
exactly? We both agreed: Not much. His game, minus a million in action, had just gotten a little bit less interesting.

Charles Town, West Virginia

Dogpatch Girls, RNGs, and Revenue Redistribution

The countryside is pretty enough, somewhat rolling, the Blue
Ridge Mountains giving off their smoky glow in the distance.
The apple orchards, what's left of them now, go back long
enough that George Washington's brother may have surveyed
their acreage. Certainly he surveyed Charles Town, a burg
that took his handle and which, by way of gratitude, named
many of the streets after his relatives, distant and otherwise. If
you're inclined, you can even visit their final resting spots in
the Zion Episcopal Cemetery.

Or you can ramble down the freshly paved Washington
Street and stare at the red courthouse where John Brown was
tried. Or ramble a little farther to see where he was hanged.
Or . . . well, that's about it. You really have no business here
unless you're a Civil War buff, are looking for alternative
housing in the pricey DC-Baltimore corridor (the orchards
are mostly divided into quarter-acre tracts now, a cheap if
ungodly commute from the nearest city), or you've somehow
gotten lost in the West Virginia panhandle, the tip of the state
that's more bedroom community these days than Appalachian
Gateway.

Unless, of course, you happen to enjoy that particular syncopation of luck unique to the rhythmic push and pull of the

slot machine. Because, baby, has this place got slot machines. Thousands of them, three floors of them, all themes, every denomination, so much colored glass and animation and nerve-jangling sound that you might as well be in Las Vegas itself. At the Charles Town Races and Slots, where an ancient (if upgraded) horse track offers the rather convoluted excuse for legalized casino gambling, there is a nearly full-blown betting experience plopped amid battlefields and subdivisions, far from what we presume to be the capitals of chance. On weekends the customers sit cheek-by-jowl at the thirty-eight hundred terminals of largely irrational hope, the place a jingling cacophony of Double Diamonds, Super Cherries, and Chop Sueys. Try to get a seat Saturday night. You can't. Many (George) Washingtons are processed in a vague, though mathematically impossible, actuarial wistfulness. Not that far from those remaining apple orchards.

No matter where I go, in other words, I can get action. Las Vegas, yeah. The back nine, sure. Utah, why not? If you don't think this country likes to gamble, well, try and find a place where you can't. So here I am, straining to find some bucolic ideal, some antique every-town that harkens back to our founding father's principles and traditions, and I find . . . a casino.

Well, for political purposes it's actually called a racino, although you'd be hard-pressed to find any difference on your own. A racino has become a budgetary expediency these days, perhaps even a civic necessity. A gold mine, for sure. And there's one coming to an apple orchard, battlefield, or cemetery near you. These days, in this country, there's no piece of scenery so sacrosanct that it can't be carved into some kind of gambling emporium, is what Charles Town teaches us. Whether it's just public appetite, a governmental burden that simply can't be shifted to taxes for fear of lost votes, or the gradual relaxation of moral authority—gambling has gone mainstream, high end and down country, all at once. It does not take a *Lonely Planet Guide to American Dissolution* to find each and every outlet for franchised sin; there's one right here in the Smokies, dolled up in strained legality and community sanction. If it makes everyone feel better to call it a racino, that's just fine.

Almost any town desperate enough can have one just like Charles Town's. This is a particular way, in a particular place, of managing law, religion, and community into the acceptance of an old social bugaboo. But it's happening everywhere, all the time, somehow. Wherever you live, assuming you don't already have access to the insane magic of random number generators (you may know them as slot machines), there is likely somebody plotting for the rehabilitation of, just for an example, a failing racetrack into a thriving casino—first video lottery terminals, then slots, finally table games as well, until you've got your own little Las Vegas.

Don't believe it? It turns out it is only a little more difficult in actuality than it was theatrically, when the visionary Hedley Lamarr first coaxed the governor to sign a bill converting the state hospital for the mentally ill to the "Wm. J. LePetomaine Memorial Gambling Casino for the Insane." That was from the movie *Blazing Saddles*, not quite a documentary but an eerie foreshadowing all the same. No real lip-smacking governor today strays all that far from Mel Brooks's character, who took up the cause with righteous gusto: "This is a giant step forward in the treatment of the insane gambler."

Gambling, given the proper geography, can be the kind of revenue source that bails out entire states. In West Virginia, where a population of 1.8 million struggles to fund the state budget, taxes on gambling address what would be more than a $300 million shortfall. In other words, behind sales tax and personal income tax, Charles Town Races and Slots (along with three other, less-producing properties in the state) is West Virginia's go-to guy when it comes to paving roads, paying teachers, or fighting fires. It's at least a giant step forward in the treatment of deficit spending.

And so, we visit historical Charles Town, looking for a glimpse into our future, doing our own survey, though not as completely as Charles Washington did three centuries ago. What would he make of this? What do I? I roam the casino property, trying to find fault with whatever premise turns pastures into parking lots, meadows into a slot floor. But, inasmuch as I'm looking at the future, I'm obliged to check my knee-jerk disapproval. There are a lot of people here, and they seem to be having a kind of fun.

The casino—not called that, of course—is tucked down a long drive off the main drag, so apart from the town that it's possible to disown it entirely if you're of a certain religious or political inclination, as some are always bound to be. When it comes to gambling, particularly in a heartland community like this, it can be amusing to parse the local ambivalence. Out of sight, out of mind, in this case.

Once inside, though, you pretty much have to come to grips with the idea that this little town has become a player in our new industry of luck. There's no getting around that. Lights are flashing, wheels are spinning, jingles are playing—and quarters are dropping.

Charles Town's casino—let's agree to call it what it is—is ruled by the same unforgiving and unseen algorithms that operate in every successful house of chance. In that respect, it's no different than any Las Vegas casino, which ought to be a surprise for everybody who's always considered our nation's gambling to be rigidly restricted, difficult to access, pretty hard to enjoy. Yet here it is, right off the turnpike, its horse track a shrewd subterfuge for a little town's gambling jones.

As I enter the casino and adjust to the computer-generated coin-drop soundtrack, I marvel, as always, at the antiquity of today's slots player. On a weekday, anyway, this must be a retiree haven, more surviving female than male, more like a diorama of mankind's inevitable decline than devil's play-ground, really. All races are represented, and upper income levels as well. I have been asked by casino management, which does not like to be portrayed as predator of the poor in the popular press, to take note of the makes and models stacked in the multiple-level parking structure as I arrive. It's true; the caliber of machinery speaks to a middle-class comfort level, even its exact age level: There are a lot of Cadillacs and Grand Marquises (not called GrandMas for nothing). But mostly—back to this again—I'm struck by the absurdly incomplete representation of man's timeline. I'm not sure I'd like to be in the casino business but I wouldn't mind having the oxygen concession here.

Still, it's not an unpleasant environment, or even particu-larly unholy. The layout is comfortable and modern, without the kind of shabbiness that might make you second-guess your choice of recreation too much. There's a food court, a gift shop, some Hollywood motifs—posters of Alfred Hitch-cock and Clark Gable—Muzak. It's not unlike an airport, really.

But this arrangement is so specifically tuned to modern life, the moral give-and-take that's our reality these days, that it's not so much a senior-citizen pit stop (baby boomers bulg-ing in the gambling pipeline right behind them; they show up weekends) as a nearly perfect economic machine. It's a model of revenue redistribution, at the heart of it, which seems to work even better than our ramshackle methods of taxation. In the ceaseless shuffling of oldsters, whose remaining futures let's hope are already provided for, there is the motion of wealth, a backward flow of money over the generations. You might even look at Charles Town Races and Slots and see a sort of enforced and mostly painless inheritance tax.

I talked to enough players—in the Western-themed OK Corral, in Slots City—that I was for the most part reassured that their heirs would not be terribly disappointed at the reading of wills. They'd be missing buckets of quarters here and there; about 2 percent of them, the statistic usually assigned to problem gamblers, might be minus a windfall altogether and, in addition, might have to put Grandma up in her final years and suffer her bitching about a near miss on a *Wheel of Fortune* progressive the entire time. But I couldn't uncover much possibility of damage in Nickelville, where the folks were simply killing time, five cents a line. "Something to do," was what I heard over and over. Nobody seemed to believe they were going to supplement Social Security by getting lucky on The Big Cheese. They had at least, after all this time, lost that capacity to fool themselves.

They were performing miracles on others' behalf, mostly. All their nickels, and quarters, and even pennies (there are $5 machines, too) are mechanically transformed into jurisdictional surpluses, with an odd payout here and there to interrupt the alchemy and keep the old-timers coming back. These coins—we're speaking metaphorically here; with ticket-in ticket-out machines, you no longer need to soil your hands with minted currency—get tossed in a really big bucket and then West Virginia can more properly attend to its infrastructure. And Jefferson County can buy an ambulance and Charles Town can put new curbs in downtown. The police chief over in Ranson, one of five municipalities in Jefferson County that receive weekly payouts from the slots, once submitted his budget and, by way of rebuke, got $50,000 more than he asked for. He won't do that again.

Maybe I forgot to tell you how big that bucket is. The

magical grind of the slots produces a near effortless 8 percent return—what these customers seem to recognize as the acceptable price of indoor fun—and before you know it (well, after a year anyway), you've got an extra third of a billion dollars. The folks who keep the lights on at Charles Town Races and Slots don't even need that much from the bucket to keep going. They're do-gooders, is what they are. They're satisfied to scrape just 45 percent of their hold—before taxes, expenses—to remain operational. The rest goes to the state lottery commission (30 percent), tourism (3 percent), the horsemen, breeders, and racing commission (16.5 percent), to veterans and pensions (1.5 percent), Jefferson County (2 percent), and to the pool of five towns within the county (2 percent). It's hard not to exult over so much found money. Every week the local newspaper, the *Journal*, runs a front-page box tallying each town's take. The week I was there, Ranson and Charles Town each pocketed $20,000 and the county received $58,000.

How big that bucket is: Operating with just those thirty-eight hundred slots (seven hundred more had been approved in 2004), the Charles Town property had a hold—its 8 percent—that year of nearly $200 million. In other words, our players (widows and retirees, as far as I could see), put $2.26 billion into those slots and, after $2.07 billion settled back into the (metaphoric) till, there was still $190.4 million left. After the above distributions—so much civic responsibility—there was nearly $80 million left. The owner, Penn National, declared more than $75 million of that as profit. Penn National, which you had never heard of until just now, and which owns thirteen additional properties (though none as successful as Charles Town's), has been one of the nation's one hundred fastest-growing companies for the last four years.

Now, maybe in addition to a scooter franchise (why do so many slots players need alternative locomotion?), you'd like to have your own racino after all. We said there were hoops to jump through, remember? First you have to make it legal, which, in these less-puritan times, is only a little tougher than Hedley Lamarr made it seem in the movie. There are technicalities you can exploit and, presuming you're not trying to get a racino up and running in the Bible Belt, there are plenty of arguments at the ready. And even if religious opposition to gambling is a problem, your referendum the source material for Sunday sermons throughout the holy commonwealth, you're not entirely out of luck. History has shown that religion can be pliable and surely can be overcome in the face of economic need (what state has enough money?), or at least tremendous opportunity.

Certainly West Virginia was not for it from the get-go. And certainly Charles Town wasn't, but it was hard for the local government to be too self-righteous, as they'd been milking the local horse track for seventy years. It was just one of those regional tracks, popular enough in the old days that a spur of railroad track was dedicated to it, delivering formally dressed sportsmen from Baltimore and Washington. Old pictures show the crowd at the rail—men in hats; it was that era—so thick "you couldn't swing a stick," says Roger Ramey, a member of the horse-racing commission that was hired by the casino to transition the conversion. "It was the thing to do then. We had Mickey Rooney, J. Edgar Hoover . . ."

The track was easily justified in the community, as any track was anywhere else, by the sheer elegance of horse racing, the sport of kings, as you well know. By the history of it, too. "This has been horse country since 1700," Mary Via told me. Via, director of the local chamber of commerce, admits that the pari-mutuel version didn't come along until the thirties, but the addition of gambling didn't trouble her "sleepy little town" all that much. In fact, the track became a principal employer, not just of the horsemen who traveled the circuit, but of townspeople as well. As recently as the 1960s, Via was typical, a kid selling tickets, making $3 on summer nights. Her father, equally typical in the community, took a second job there. "Everybody had second jobs there." The track was a tightly woven thread in the community fabric.

But the track, as any track anywhere else, was becoming an increasingly threadbare fabric by the mid-eighties. A tax change in 1986 that blasted write-offs for breeders right out of the tax code reduced margins. But also there was the introduction of state lotteries. Horse racing was no longer the only place to bet a bob. And, too, simulcast racing reduced the need to attend live events. All these developments contributed to the quality of horse racing as well as attendance. Smaller purses produced fields of substandard horseflesh. And with weaker racing, attendance declined even more.

West Virginia recognized a way to save the industry, and fill its pockets as well. Notice how big ideas, much like Chicago fog, creep in on little cat feet. In 1990 its lottery commission got a law passed, which allowed a similarly failing track in Chester, Mountaineer Park, to install 165 lottery terminals. Four years later it approved slots for all four tracks in the state, forcing an agreement for an amazing 60 percent of the take, some of which would be directed to the improvement of facilities, breeding, and general quality of racing. Why not save a dying business, was the reasoning. And pave some roads . . .

Of course, the state was simply offering a way out here. It was up to each county to decide if it wanted slots. And in Jefferson County, in 1994, nobody did.

The voters were morally opposed, not so much to gambling but to more gambling. Plus, they were wary of the consortium that was pushing the conversion. The first vote failed by a two-to-one margin. But two years later, with the track in such serious decline that, according to Ramey, the ownership group was fixing to declare bankruptcy and sell it for a housing development, it was a different matter. It helped that Penn National, which was a small-fry horse-racing company at heart, stepped in with a far more believable platform of promises. It said, if it could get slots inside, it would completely rebuild the facility, retain a workforce without any interruption in employment, and restore racing to its gloried past, although it couldn't promise to bring Hoover back.

Penn National was a canny lobbyist. The vote passed two-to-one in 1996; Penn National completed the purchase the next year and, in addition to the immediate installation of 450 video lottery terminals (VLTs—slot-machine starter kits, basically), really did begin a massive upgrading of the facility. It's easy to be cynical, in that the company, for all its roots in the industry, wasn't really that interested in horse racing when it plunged in with its $18 million purchase. But it immediately spent $56 million on remodeling everything from kitchens to lights to the turf itself. And it keeps spending, even beyond the portions of its tax that get directed to the sport. Seven years later it was still building barns and regrading the track. The upshot was that horse racing in Charles Town, even if it doesn't pull its own weight, is healthy again. Purses that once were $22,000 a day for nine races are now $200,000 a day for eleven or twelve races. The horseflesh is, once more, several grades above glue.

As I discovered, however, the relationship between the casino and the track is strictly a technicality. One of the state's provisions is that both properties must remain contiguous, so that the tracks won't become orphaned by the property's real raison d'être. At Charles Town, this means that, to travel between the two, you must negotiate a long and strange and sloping hallway. Awkward. But, then, whom are we kidding? Nobody actually travels between the two. The rejuvenation of horse racing in Charles Town is sweet, in a quaint and historical way, but it's largely pointless, entirely political. Penn National clearly intends to continue subsidizing the racing, and good for it. But the company, no matter what its origins, couldn't care less if a casino customer ever finds that hallway. Here, over here, here's where the slots are.

At Charles Town, the original VLTs still occupy a section of the casino, but it feels more like a museum than anything else. For folks used to playing the state lottery these primitive machines were a nice transition to casino gambling. But for folks used to casino gambling (Atlantic City's not that far away after all), they weren't anything to justify a day-trip. Charles Town wasn't able to put in real coin-out slots until the end of 1999. It hasn't stopped adding machines and it doesn't plan on stopping. And why would it? Each machine it installs leverages the bottom line. According to some figures, a West Virginia slot machine "holds" more than $200 a day (much more than that at Charles Town). This compares to Nevada, where the daily profit per unit is something like $85. So, yeah, clear the decks. More machines!

If this business model seems tempting, you should know that you need to overcome more than politics in your racino start-up. Charles Town is blessed with, more than anything, a very lucky geography. These people inserting their Players' Choice cards into Jackpot Party are not from West Virginia, hardly. Only 4 percent of the visitors are in-state. The rest come from DC and Baltimore. Charles Town Races and Slots, which seems in the middle of nowhere, is actually in the middle of everywhere. It has access to one of the largest markets in the country; within a hundred miles of pretty good freeway is a population of about 10 million people.

The other thing you might like to ensure, if you at all can, is a monopoly. There is no legalized gambling in Maryland or Virginia, two states that account for nearly 70 percent of the casino's visitors. Pennsylvania, which has been lusting

after the racino money, only in 2004 passed legislation allowing it, but it will need start-up time. So, West Virginia has
had gambling all to itself. But monopolies are not forever,
and today's easy money can disappear in a single referendum.
Pennsylvania accounts for only 16 percent of the Charles
Town fan base, so a racino at Pocono Downs is not a big
problem (and not a problem at all for Penn National, which
operates the facility). But now Maryland . . . with a nearly
$2 billion deficit, and some dying tracks, that could be a
disaster for Charles Town. There is a nice movement afoot to
get slots into tracks much closer to Baltimore and Washington, to keep those Maryland dollars at home, to bolster its
own thoroughbred industry, to pave its own roads. It's just a
matter of time, really.

Charles Town officials are confident their entrenchment,
their infrastructure, their loyal customer base will amount to
substantial advantage in the face of what will be, at first anyway, a halting competition. For the moment, they don't even
bus people in, or put them up once they've arrived; the pick-
ings are so easy there's no need to dilute the revenue stream
with expensive marketing. But nobody pretends the bottom
line will hold up if there's more than one game in town. And
it's too good a game not to get into.

Of course, it's not really a game at all, is it? What makes this
work for (almost) everybody is not politics or geography but
the application of technology, low and high, to that most fundamental of human traits—wishful thinking. It so happens
that the slot machine, which is what racinos and even casinos
are all about at heart, is a particularly devilish device when it
comes to targeting and exploiting man's capacity for hope.
There's no invention in the world like it for the excitement of
success in the continued and guaranteed expression of failure.
You're going to lose; you have to lose. You do lose. And yet,

given our destiny to pluck jackpots out of thin air, it would simply be irresponsible to not bet again. Of this basic impulse have nest eggs been diminished, and empires built.

The first machines, built in the 1890s, only a little bit after designers first developed a coin-vending technology, played on the recent Gold Rush phenomenon, during which it had become acceptable and occasionally profitable to play long odds. In fact, the initial craze was almost entirely limited to San Francisco, where the get-rich vapors were still part of the everyday atmosphere. The machines, whether they were built on wheel or poker or three-reel platforms, were sometimes ornate and beautiful, but always (then as now) deviously effective at the mathematical manipulation of small change. Customers at cigar shops and bars might have reasonably supposed the machines were closely tied to retail marketing; they often awarded drinks, cigars, or other prizes (the familiar fruit tokens—lemons, cherries—actually represented chewing gum flavors). Yet manufacturers were fully aware of the machines' actual promise and quickly established a thriving industry in the Bay Area. By the turn of the century, developing its iron-age version of Silicon Valley, San Francisco was home to the Monarch Card Machine Company, Royal Card Machine, Charles Fey & Company, C. R. Light Company, and more.

They were crude, gear-driven instruments of amusement, dependent entirely for their enormous profits on the simple if absurd proposition of taking in more coins than they paid out. This, as far as the customer is concerned, is a losing proposition, of course, and hardly anybody who played those slots, even in those early days, could have imagined the machines were gaffed to the consumers' advantage. But the makers had unknowingly tapped into a powerful psychology, exploiting man's necessary acceptance of defeat in pursuit of eventual success. The folks at Mills Novelty may not have understood the Skinnerian principles of behavior, but they certainly were applying them in the design of Klondike, a rather addictive apparatus that rewarded—intermittently—certain, otherwise ridiculous, behaviors. Like putting a nickel in a wooden piece of furniture and pulling a handle, and hoping for the best.

It is only recently in gambling's history that the slot machine has been restored to its prominence on the casino floor. For years real gambling meant table games, bookies, the greased wheels of roulette. The slot machine, which demanded no decision-making beyond the initial act of sitting in front of one, was considered the dumbest appliance of chance in the joint. This is where wives got parked, bankrolled with a tub of quarters, while menfolk went about the real business of bringing down the house.

The casino industry eventually discovered that these untended machines, dialed in to produce a set profit, were generating all the income. They didn't know exactly why—psychiatrists do; it's called the intermittent schedule of reinforcement—but they didn't exactly care. The $100 black-jack player is relatively expensive to maintain; he requires a dealer, pit boss, security, floor real estate and—worse!—he sometimes wins. The quarter slots player, on the other hand, is a virtual lab rat, easily trained to dump change into a machine that is programmed to return slightly less, in exchange for the experience.

Nancy Petrie, who teaches psychiatry at the University of Connecticut School of Medicine, marvels at the mostly unrecognized genius of the slot machine, what she calls the near-perfect exploitation of human behavior. "The idea that you may or may not get a reward," she told me, "that shapes a very powerful behavior." She's found that rats can be trained, through the principle of intermittent reinforcement, to "actually prefer riskier behavior, gravitating toward the very big payoff options, even as the odds go lower." Is this a behavior that humans might emulate? She laughed, quite a bit actually.

The casinos did not need to commission any studies to discover this on their own, or even read up on the studies that Petrie and her colleagues conduct. They have their own lab set up and, to the extent that they can count money (can they ever!), can easily perform their own experiments on human behavior. What they've found is that slot machines, with their ability to provide second-order conditioning (when bells are going off nearby) and the near-win phenomenon (the third cherry doesn't quite line up), create an incredibly loyal and determined and rich source of income. Today, slots represent 70 percent of their gambling revenue.

And, as political encouragement has replaced moral approbation, they've become even more important to the industry. When states dip their toes into gambling waters, it is first and perhaps only to introduce slot machines. In West Virginia, legislators so far have found it unnecessary to add the unwieldy and less profitable table games to their gambling repertoire. In Pennsylvania, where they voted to chase those same recreational dollars that have been leaking over the state line, the game of choice will again be slot machines—sixty-one thousand of them, all over Pennsylvania.

The slot machine is no longer a crude, gear-driven hunk of hope. Now that slots take in more than $30 billion in North America—more than three times what our citizens spend on movie tickets, for one example—there has been what you might call a technological sophistication brought to bear. The industry is huge, highly competitive, and fiendishly inventive. As a consequence, what you see on a casino floor today, bubbling and burping away, is easily the finest-tuned extractor of cash on the planet.

Today's slot machine makes the casino experience perfectly reproducible. What has been working in Las Vegas all these years will absolutely work in Charles Town. It allows a kind of franchising, whereby a day at the casino is reliably generic—as much fun (or not) in West Virginia as it ever was in Nevada. Just buy some product off the shelf and you're good to go. No reinventing the wheel here. No spinning it, either.

If you really want to understand how gambling became so transportable—how a Civil War town in the boondocks can become a regional hotbed for slots hobbyists—you ought to understand the machines themselves, which are the heart of the experience. Hanging around the Charles Town slots floor, even talking to behavioral psychiatrists, only explained so much. To penetrate the entertainment interface, to get past the end user's rhythmic push and pull. And for that, you really do need to go to Las Vegas.

Days after leaving West Virginia, I visited the G2E, Global Gaming Expo at the Las Vegas Convention Center, which is a sort of new car show for the gambling industry. Manufacturers of everything from card shufflers to surveillance systems annually trot out their wares for inspection by casino executives. Although you could visit to see what's new in the world of casino database management, you probably wouldn't. Of the twenty-six thousand that showed up for the three-day affair, all but one or two were there to see what new slots IGT or WMS or Aristocrat Technologies had thought up. It was about the slots, totally.

I had no idea what to expect. But even if I'd been told I was entering the seventh circle of hell, I still would not have been prepared for the fever dream that had been organized here. Most of the quarter-million square feet had been set aside for slots manufacturers, and the competing madness of so many beeping, clanging, coin-rattling machines was so overwhelming that the only possible frames of reference were either spiritual or pharmaceutical. The full effect of several thousand fully lit, mostly animated slot machines in full "attract" mode, clamoring for attention like so many computerized orphans, reminded you of either a religious experience or a full-blown hallucination, assuming you believe there's a difference.

I had to recoil from the assault, regain equilibrium. Meanwhile I noticed that the other attendees had not been made as queasy at the sight of so much perverted ingenuity. Upon raising the overhead doors at the one p.m. official opening, there had been a land rush of slot managers, casino execs, tribal chiefs, gaming analysts. The surge was nearly frightening. Before I could gather my tote bag of promotional materials, almost all the machines—which were playing freely—had been thronged and were dinging in full throat. Casually uniformed software designers appeared to walk the "players" through the game, explaining bonus rounds, progressives, hit rates. It did not contribute to my shifting sense of reality to see a gang of Dogpatch girls giving booth-babe flourishes to a game called Hee-Haw, which promised a quarter-million-dollar jackpot, if not an actual Dogpatch girl.

These were all prototypes, new editions, rethought ideas. Not all of them would wow casino buyers, or ever make it to a casino floor, and even so, the winners among them would still need jurisdictional approval before even a penny could be passed through them. As such, these were mostly concept machines but, to the degree that even a few of them would grow up to supplant more familiar machines, like Double Diamonds, it was a look into the future.

If so, this is what it's going to look like: There's going to be a lot of top boxes with giant touch-screens and stereo sound, all animated by a demographically appropriate spokesperson. And they're going to be so complicated, requiring actual decisions even, and with such heroic story lines embedded in a narrative experience that, supposing you do learn how to play them, you'll never be able to leave.

I wandered the floor, taking in a potpourri of pop culture

that seems to have become the protective coloration of gambling these days. Designers make no secret of their desire to establish a demographic affinity with players, and so plunder movies, TV shows, and even infomercials for strands of familiarity, anything that might rope somebody in. So, I saw machines based on almost every *Saturday Night Live* sketch ever written—even the Coneheads. There was a Back to the Future game, Elvis games, a Beverly Hillbillies game (Cash for Crude!), games based on *Laverne & Shirley*, Regis Philbin, and Elizabeth Taylor (her Dazzling Diamonds machine dispensed real jewelry in the bonus rounds).

The manufacturers, who must license these properties, seem to abide by no particular guidelines when it comes to picking their figureheads. I saw so much scattershot celebrity that it was impossible to figure out any behavioral strategies when it came to assigning fame to a machine. In one day there I saw—in the flesh—Drew Carey, Clint Eastwood, Pamela Anderson, Pelé, and Ron Popeil. Except for Carey, who was taking abnormal interest in his Big Ball of Cash machine, the celebrities seemed to be seeing their branded game for the first time that day. Eastwood was prodded toward his Fistful of Dollars machine during the game's unveiling and, although he seemed delighted (why wouldn't he be—licensing fees are said to exceed $1 million), he was definitely clueless. "What do I do?" he asked one of the designers.

There were a lot of machines that read much more like a video game than a slot, with magical elements and mystical scenarios, directed (somewhat) by interaction with a touch screen. There were multiplying levels of bonus rounds, with increasing complexity but also entertainment value, if not odds. I tried to play Popeil's Showtime Rotisserie machine, which was gaffed to send me right into the bonus round, even though I didn't know what I was doing. Moreover, I had no idea what kind of money I might be playing for but I was thrilled to see that I had advanced far enough that an on-screen Popeil was offering me a choice of turkey injection—pineapple, garlic, you name it. The *CSI*-style animation showed a rather grisly shot of pineapple being forced into turkey flesh and then a quick screen shot of an infomercial audience cheering wildly. Would I pay a quarter to see that again? Absolutely!

It was clear to me that the industry, by way of apology almost, was trying to give the player the sense that he was getting something for his money—a mini-show, a few laughs, a little nostalgia (I mean, *Bewitched*?). But it wasn't clear to me that the player was going to care all that much. I enjoyed the spectacle and I appreciated the effort being made to overcome the irrefutable logic of slots play, but I doubted it mattered.

When I returned to the casino that night—which hardly differed, now that I thought about it, from its West Virginia cousin—I was surprised to see that the busiest machines were still the old standbys, three-reel machines that play like an old-fashioned one-arm bandit. Not that the top-box machines didn't have their devotees. But it occurred to me that nobody was pumping nickels into these machines because they enjoyed watching Bill Cosby and Robert Culp in *I Spy* thirty years ago. They were doing it because they thought they were going to win.

They can't, they won't. The random number generator, which is producing outcomes by the nanosecond (and entirely independent of any action you take), makes sure of that. This little device dictates specific results over the long run, while accommodating erratic events in the short run. There might be two huge jackpots in a row, you never know. But over the life of the machine, it will keep a prescribed portion of each dollar (at least 75 cents, but more like 92 in competitive markets such as Las Vegas casino floors) for he who owns it. Machines that might cost as much as a subcompact car can consequently be amortized in a matter of months, especially if, in noncompetitive markets like West Virginia, each machine holds more than $200 every day. Every day of its winking, blinking life. It adds up.

Still, it is no great trick to program the illusion of possibility into every machine. This is not done by licensing the Blues Brothers' likenesses but by tinkering with volatility, offering players choices between high-frequency-but-low-paying machines and low-frequency-mega-jackpot machines. It might take some doing to get a $1 million jackpot out of a 25-cent stand-alone machine (at least one that doesn't take four hundred years of steady play to produce) but this is where numbers come out to play. It can be done, and the very notion of a payoff, no matter how remote, is what keeps the rats pushing the levers.

Of course some do win. There is a weirdly determined subset of gambler who has identified video poker—sort of a slot machine—as the one advantage play in a casino. Indeed, most casinos maintain at least several machines capable of 100-percent-plus returns in this wildly addictive game. But only if played perfectly. And even when that's possible (each game must be solved on computers, apart from the general rules of poker), the advantage is so small that to play it profitably must seem like the worst kind of line work. I talked with the pseudonymous Bob Dancer, author of *Million Dollar Video Poker*, and he presented a rather unglamorous picture of the professional life. A former software guy who moved to Las Vegas in 1993, Dancer was for some reason determined to make it as a gambler. He did make it, to the point where, as he says, he's set for life. But it meant collecting coupons, fun-books, taking part in players clubs, cashing in $50 checks from casinos anxious for his tremendous coin-in totals.

Dancer told me there might be one hundred players like him, who earn a living this way, making $60,000 a year or so.

Dancer, who publishes a Las Vegas newspaper column identifying perks and promotions in the local casinos, is mostly drawn to the puzzle-solving aspect of the life, although he admits he does have some gamble in him. In any case, he finds that he spends five to ten hours a day in smoky rooms, playing video poker machines as fast as he can, running as much as $30,000 an hour through a $50 machine. This is in expectation, though not absolute assurance, of earning $50 an hour.

Dancer and his peers do better working the players clubs. He wins cars, cruises, mugs, cashbacks, you name it, just on the basis of his play. And he can get lucky. The title of his book was made possible when, playing a $25 machine, he hit a royal flush for $100,000 and his wife, playing a $100 machine, hit one a half hour later for $400,000. Mostly, though, it's just grinding away, exploiting a percentage point in a Deuces Wild game here, an exorbitant promotion in a players club there. When I spoke with Dancer toward the end of 2004, just back from a Mexican cruise a casino had awarded him, he admitted that after averaging $75,000 in winnings the past two years, he was at zero for the most recent one. "But," he pointed out, "there's a full week left in 2004. Anything can happen."

The "anything" that gamblers refer to is the life-changing event of such astronomical odds that participation is close to irrelevant. The MegaJackpots system, which is linked in a giant multistate network to make huge payouts possible, seems to click in regularly enough, once every ten days or so, to make the good life seem extremely possible. Yet, just as it takes some eight thousand machines working together to pony up a $4 million payday, so does it take a lot of community pulls—say 15 million of them—to produce that single statistical certainty. Even if a player gets the industry average ten spins a minute—six hundred games an hour—it would take a certain dedication to outlast the random number generator on his own. Let's face it, the chances of hitting it big, with the IGT folks (who own the machine, in this case) suddenly appearing with the winner's kit (you know, the novelty check) are about the same whether you play the game or you don't.

But like our psychiatrist said, if an animal is exposed to a lot of unpredictable environments its whole life, it might come to prefer riskier choices, where the chance of a larger payoff is possible, especially with modest investments. Could this apply to humans in a casino? Nancy Petrie had laughed when I asked her that. "You know, up here in Connecticut, we do have the largest casino in the country . . ." Her very own lab.

It got me thinking back to the G2E, where about half of the machines I saw were what casinos call multi-denoms, that is, neither quarter nor dollar machines but capable of almost any level of denomination. It used to be that casinos offered the nickel machines as a kind of pregambler grooming, hoping to graduate the player to the dollar machines. But they've discovered an even better way to hijack his self-control. They've gone back to penny machines, which offer the illusion of disciplined investment (a penny, for God's sake), coupled with the usual expensive-looking array of graphics, "sound events," narrative bonus rounds, and huge payoffs (and not in piles of objectionable copper, thanks to the coinless technology). And, most important, or rather insidious, they've given the player the ability to play multi-lines, offering as many as thirty different opportunities to group winning symbols. If all thirty are chosen (and they pretty much have to be, to offer the player his highest potential), the zigzag pattern looks like a Congressional redistricting; but no longer must the player suffer the heartbreak of a near miss. He is covered.

The upshot is, a penny machine, with a max bet of five cents, and thirty different betting lines, now plays—not like a nickel machine, a quarter machine, or even a dollar machine—exactly like a $1.50 machine. The player may not notice at first, because the machine can be programmed to have a hit frequency of anywhere from 37 percent to 50, which is nice action. The rattle of coins, even if it's a simulated and somewhat fattened digital sound burst, is not considered to be terribly discouraging. Remember our psychiatrist's description of "second-order conditioning"?

And what the machine can't do on its own, the casino can. It has the ability to track every machine on the floor and, thanks to the use of player club cards (inserted in the slot machine so the player can qualify for comps and other promotions), it can track the play of every customer as well. At Harrah's, where this linked technology has been used first and most extensively, it might mean that a "luck ambassador" from the casino will suddenly appear at the side of a distraught loser, both to commiserate and share some casino swag to buck his spirits up. Or, at the Borgata in Atlantic City, it might mean the machine magically dispenses slot dollars to incentivize customers during slow times. A cash voucher, a free buffet, a bobblehead doll, a slot dollar from nowhere, and the player is back in business.

But there is no free buffet, not really. The machine's steady grind will sooner or later exhaust every player's bankroll, and no luck ambassador in the world is going to change that. Because here's the thing: Behind all that colored glass, streaming video, gripping story lines, and appealing nostalgia is the unrepentant logic of the random number generator. It is set to produce the guaranteed erosion—8 percent, over and over, until further calculation becomes unnecessary—of the player's pathetic bucket of nickels. Now, the player may not mind—the old folks in Charles Town certainly didn't seem to. They were simply paying for a little excitement, their extra coins happily forfeited in the continued expression of hopefulness. It can even be fun. But the statistical probability that governs the life of a slot machine is incorruptible, not so vulnerable to man's ambition. The little machine just sits there, beeping and burping, its hidden algorithms producing one of the most perfect and effortless profit centers known to man.

Is it any wonder that everybody wants some of their own? I get a daily roundup of gambling news, which is heavy on industry minutiae and backroom busts, but which almost always has a feature from some state politician angling for legalized gambling. It solves so many problems, so easily. A lot of these stories are dispatches from gambling's border wars, as states try to compete for slots dollars just across the line. In the 2004 election, there were battle thrusts of some magnitude or other in twenty-five states, as the Pennsylvanias of this country began going after the West Virginias.

Sometimes the stories are far more specific, as if general budget woes were not convincing enough for the debate. Recently, the city of Indianapolis, which was already sporting a deficit of $600 million, announced an agreement with its NFL franchise, the Colts, to finance a $500 million retractable-roof stadium to keep the wandering team in place. Of that amount, $100 million would come from the Colts and the NFL. The rest, $400 million, the city said would come from slot machines, most of which had yet to be authorized.

Some of these proposals sound unrealistic, to say the least. They do not acknowledge the possibility of saturation, unrealistic taxation, or the next new thing. The urge to gamble may be powerful, but is not so all-consuming that it will demolish all obstacles to it. Even in the struggle for competing vices, gambling is not always a sure shot: Delaware racinos were rolling along, just like West Virginia's, until the state instituted a smoking ban and, while its neighbor experienced 38 percent growth, its nonsmoking business plummeted 11 percent. And elsewhere states have found that unlimited expansion is not always profitable, especially when politics make the payoff so unpredictable. Illinois got a little greedy in 2004, raised the incremental gaming rate to 70 percent, and watched the industry tank as the governmental overhead simply proved too much. Making slots work in New York, with an 80 percent rate, won't be easy, either (the state initially suggested 90 percent and the gaming industry said, thanks, no).

Still, there was an expectation coming out of the 2004 G2E confab that there'd be orders for more than 150,000 additional machines, taking the total in North America to something like 800,000 by late 2007. Worries that initiatives were meeting opposition across the country—Warren Buffett torpedoed proposals in Nebraska, the Humane Society was giving gamblers in Florida fits, and church groups in Oklahoma were battling a state lottery—were being taken seriously, of course. But the industry was mostly secure, smug even, in its ability to leverage our positive thinking, turn a colossally maladaptive reaction to failure (we're bound to win next time!) into a steadily growing income stream. And it was more certain than ever in its ability to fine-tune technology and engineer even greater rewards out of our wrong-headed regret response (we'll get it back!).

As I walked the floor in Charles Town, I found it difficult to see this big picture. I could only take in the particulars, old men with World War II battleship caps staring into the colored glass, not so much bewildered by the machines' stubbornness, their resistance to anything like luck, but just resigned. The 8-percent grind is a small price to pay for the pursuit of possibility, small change when it comes to preserving the spirit of speculation. The vestigial impulse to take a chance—which has served us all in our hopes of self-improvement, or just survival—is getting some exercise, is all. Just costs a quarter a line (max bet, 75 cents).

Not too long after I left the cheerfully clinking casino, driving back to Washington Dulles, along the smoothly paved streets of Charles Town, right out of West Virginia's newly solvent countryside, I read that the racino's owner, Penn National, had just bought Illinois-based Argosy Gaming Company, which runs riverboat casinos throughout the Midwest, for $2.2 billion, and had in the process become the nation's third-largest casino operator (behind MGM-Mirage and Harrah's). Penn National's stock had already grown sixtyfold in the last ten years, had doubled this past year. The day it happened, the stock went up $10.78 more on the news, a combined win of over $40 million for investors. A MegaJackpot, really.

Cobalt Shades, Cold Decks, and Footprints in the Data

For some gamblers, the element of chance becomes too irritating to endure. By removing it, by turning good bets into sure bets, by reducing risk to the point where a proposition doesn't so much represent an opportunity as it does income, they are able to enjoy the calm of righteous destiny. These gamblers are, in a word, cheats. They past-post, they chip-switch, they muck decks, they put down paper, dowb cards, fix fights, buy players, they juice dice. They organize odds to such complete advantage that, really, they are no longer gambling at all. They are no longer participating in that helter-skelter world of insufficient probability and incomplete information. They're just grinding out a living.

There's a moral component to this activity that they must ignore, of course, but some are so aggrieved by the ruthlessness of fortune that they are able to forgive themselves the instinct to make life a little less random. There is a legal component as well, which these gamblers can't neglect with the same carelessness. Nobody likes a cheat but nobody hates a cheat like the house. Presumably, the peace that a stripped deck provides is at least somewhat offset by the anxiety that surveillance excites. Somewhat, anyway.

There are entire crews out there, braving the gray glass bubbles in the casino ceiling, mocking the scrutiny of state enforcement. Nobody knows how many, or even how much they're getting away with. The good ones don't get caught. Every once in a while a high-profile grifter is brought down and, if he's proven felonious enough, is nominated for Nevada's Black Book (which is actually silver). That's sort of the hall of fame for cheaters, getting a statewide blackball, although in the past it has rewarded mobsters much more than it has card mechanics. In any case, it's only the sporadic intervention of authority that illuminates this little underworld.

A couple of years ago the FBI finally put Dennis McAndrew away, although it wasn't easy. McAndrew, whose career objectives were hardly secret (he'd already been convicted in a 1986 scheme to relieve slot machines of $10 million), was somehow systematically looting Las Vegas progressives. His confederates were walking out with cars, jackpots ranging from $30,000 to $3.7 million. You name it.

McAndrew, whose real name is Nikrasch, was somehow cracking the case of the slot machine and, using a handheld device, was reprogramming the random number generator to produce a hit for the next person to play it. In all, before wiretaps and informants confirmed the feds' suspicions, he and his crew made off with $6 million.

Jerry Markling, chief of Nevada's Enforcement Division, was almost admiring. "He's very good, very bright."

The slot floor has always represented a technological arms race, manufacturers trying to stay ahead, or at least keep up, with the crooks. McAndrew would need far more sophisticated means to trick a slot machine today. Stories of characters filling up their coin buckets by inserting light wands up the slot are strictly archival at this point; with ticket-in, ticket-out play the rage, there is no longer any point to fooling a counting sensor. And you hope that the Gaming Control Board will never again be bamboozled by the likes of Ronald Harris, an inspector with access to source codes, who a decade ago tricked Atlantic City keno machines into spitting out tons of nickels. His scheme was clever, beyond the routine sophistication of computer nerdiness, for forcing the machines to pay only when a prescribed sequence of coins was dropped. He didn't want to share.

There will always be somebody able to reverse-engineer one of these machines to produce a payout, although the electronics are now complex enough to rule out the sort of *Mechanics Illustrated* hobbyist that used to thwart them.

"Insiders, programmers," Markling said. "Those are the guys that concern us now." In the battle against these cheats, the knuckle-busters of yore have been replaced by computer forensic guys, their pocket protectors as scary as any of those old tools of dissuasion.

Most cheating, though, is comparatively low-tech. There certainly are crews taking down online poker rooms, with a basement full of computers representing as many as six "different" players (I've talked to one such one-man crew). And rumors of hackers getting into the site's algorithms are all over the chat rooms. But online sites, a test of faith anyway, are only as good as their security, and you can bet—in fact, you do bet!—they're battling to maintain their game's integrity. You wouldn't keep wiring your money away if you thought everybody could see your hole cards.

Poker is not known as the "cheating game" for nothing. It's been sanitized by TV packagers lately, but it will never escape its legacy as a Wild West recreation, updated only to the extent that gunplay is now relatively rare. It still attracts scammers and mechanics and it probably doesn't pay to sit in on a high-stakes game of strangers. That includes high-end Las Vegas rooms, stocked with poker-magazine cover boys, where the security is presumably tight. I talked to one rounder, whose experience as a cheat covers several disciplines and as many decades, and he rattled off a who's who of colluders, enough talent to make a WSOP final table. I was wary of his charges—he is a cheat, after all—but found some of his claims plausible enough to keep me from ever thinking of trying my luck at hi-lo.

This particular character may or may not have the goods on today's players. But his stories of a wide-open Los Angeles, when cheaters had the run of poker clubs until a *Los Angeles Times* exposé in 1982, and an equally corrupt Las Vegas in the 1970s, are entertaining if not fully sourced. It sounded authentic to me when he told me about a foray to Costa Rica, where he and his accomplices brought special inks to mark the cards and contact glasses that made the ink visible to the game. "Had glasses cloned by an optometrist," he told me, in a rambling but convincing yarn, "cobalt blue, the kind Stu Ungar wore when he won [the WSOP] in '87. Every thief saw Stewie in those glasses bet a few hundred on him. Anyway, we go down there, got the lenses, got the ruby-red ink—$500 a gram for the ink—got the top card mechanic in the world and . . . nothing works. Duped. Ink's no good. Get a hold of a guy, has better ink, sends it Western Union. Get it the next day, it's good. Win half-million right away."

Las Vegas was just as wild, he said, even when it seemed to be going legit in the eighties. "An absolute circus," he said of one of the newer card rooms. "Just blatant. Always crooked." He said he was so uncomfortable playing by their rules that he finally got demoted and was forced to leave town. "Who are you gonna complain to," he said. "There's a code you have to follow if you don't want to end up in the desert." He sounded wistful. "It was so easy to cheat. Why would you ever rob a 7-Eleven when you could play poker in Las Vegas?"

When I tell him these are all good stories but not really checkable, he flags me to a retired card mechanic in Florida, a guy who dealt in Las Vegas poker rooms in the seventies. While the mechanic didn't have special knowledge of the Costa Rica game, and while he wasn't the self-promoter his pal was, he did have his own yarns. Talking in a tired, dispirited voice, he told me of the days when "Tony the Ant" Spilotro ran games, when table security meant breathing room for roving gangs of cheats weaving in and out of games, not the tourists. "It was always crooked," he told me. "Any high-limit game, it got taken. Marked cards, cold decks, collusion, whatever it took." He mentioned the names of several high-profile players, the sort of famous gamblers who might have books out, and confirmed them as more or less deadly in their grisly influence. In fact, he said, there was a contract out on his own life after he got in a beef with a poker-room manager. "He couldn't stand me knowing everything," he said. "Barred me out of the hotel, put a contract out on me." The way he said it, it was like, what are you gonna do? "I'm still here," he reminded me.

I choose to regard these gentlemen (whom I've kindly left unnamed) as curators of another time, another game, rather than as state's evidence. Although it might be to your benefit, next time you sit in on a $100 game, a grizzled TV presence at your side, to pause for reflection before the next re-buy. Paranoia can be useful when you're dribbling away your nest egg.

In fact, paranoia ought to be the guiding instinct when it comes to most gambling. If there's an event up for grabs, there almost assuredly is somebody trying to fix it. The reminders are periodic, generally when some college basketball program gets caught in a big-money shakedown. These kids, who are essentially working for free, are ideal targets for fixers. Just shave a few points here and there—not even asking you to lose!—and you'll be rolling in dough.

It happens about once every ten years or so, as far as we know, going back to the great City College of New York scandal in the late forties. There was another one in the late fifties; a Boston College mess in the late seventies, when Henry Hill of *Goodfellas* fame got together with Richard "Richie the Fixer" Perry; another point-shaving shutdown at Tulane in the eighties; and, in 1997, an investigation into Arizona State point shaving in 1994.

The ASU scandal was scary, because it showed how easy it was. These were not criminal masterminds, either, but bumbling amateurs who didn't know better than to spread their bets around. Having favorably influenced the outcome on two games near the end of the 1994 season (they bought off two ASU guards for "tens of thousands," a campus bookie having provided the introductions), the gamblers loaded up for a final score. They stood at Las Vegas sports books, the day of their big game, with $250,000 in cash. For an ASU-Washington game? In fact, basketball being what it is, the games themselves, in which the favorites usually won, aroused no suspicions. It was the gambling that was raising red flags. In fact, the action was so strange—these particular games were being bet way out of proportion—that not only did a sports book take the game down for a time, but another gambler, who was involved in the notorious Computer Group of the eighties (a confederation of gamblers who used a program to smash the betting line and made as much as $15 million during one NFL season), phoned the NCAA to warn it of possible point shaving. These gamblers hated the idea of somebody having an edge they didn't.

And even so, the investigation into the scheme languished for three years until an informant looking to reduce his drug sentencing came forward with a little story about college basketball.

And this only happens once every ten years? Actually, according to a professor at the Wharton School, it happens all the time. Justin Wolfers, a ponytailed Australian who has demonstrated a fascination with gambling in several other studies (he comes by his fascination honestly; he worked at the tracks Down Under before becoming an academic), decided to attack the problem by imagining the kind of evidence such corruption would leave. No sense trying to identify it as it happens, but maybe it was possible to apply what he calls forensic economics to prove the aftermath.

I reached Wolfers after one of his classes in predictive markets, where he directs his students in some provocative studies. Is racial discrimination a possibility in NBA officiating? Could he prove, by looking at box scores, that Pete Rose did not bet on the Reds? In Wolfers's world, there is no such thing as a coincidence. "Ever notice," he wondered, "how often a company hits its Wall Street number?" Tracing the action backward, *CSI*-style, it's possible to prove almost anything.

What Wolfers found, after studying data from 44,120 NCAA Division I games—the kind of popular matchups that attract betting lines—was that something appeared to be very wrong. This didn't surprise him. "Think about how many resources the NCAA devotes to gambling," he said. "That should probably be telling us something." The numbers would say for certain, though. And sure enough, it seemed to him that twelve-point favorites were winning games by eleven points a lot more often than they were winning by thirteen. His analysis suggested that "point shaving *may* be quite widespread, with an indicative, albeit rough estimate that around 6 percent of strong favorites have been willing to manipulate their performance." In other words, the "footprints in the data" told him that about five hundred games in his sixteen-year sample must have been fixed.

The real question is not that five hundred games are fixed. The question is: Did you bet on one of them?

Santa Ynez, California

Powwows, Jackpots, and Lynch Mobs

Topping San Marcos Pass, coming from the California coastline near Santa Barbara, offers the motorist a shock of scenery, a sudden valley of sere grasses below him, spotted with distant oaks, all framed by violent slabs of sheer sandstone. There aren't many vistas to compare. The gently folded ravines of the valley floor are in such contrast to the seismic upheaval beyond—sharp tiers of mountain, one after the other, still crackling the earth's crust in their geological adolescence— that the first reaction is a kind of confusion. How exactly does this fit together? In the winters, when the rains do not wash out the twisting Route 154, the motorist sees a landscape gone to green, the chalky cliffs offering a muted relief. In summer, the scrubby oaks, with their broccoli tops, are all that punctuate the tanned valley floor beneath. Late in the day, as the sun sets behind foothills to the west, the bouldered Santa Ynez Mountains glow purple.

The San Marcos Pass is part of a thirty-two-mile byway, a breathtaking shortcut up the California coast. You could easily remain on Highway 101, a four-lane highway that runs up and down the state, and feel just as embarrassed by the scenic surplus. Surf on one side, mountain ranges on the other; sloping pastures here, gorges there; stands of pine, remorseless stretches of rock. But the pass, which cuts off the more manageable curve of the 101 as it heads inland and up into the San Joaquin Valley, is such a spectacular concentration of Western icons, accentuated by its absurd changes in elevation, that it ought to be required travel for anyone who wants a taste of the West and, for some reason, has only thirty-two miles in him.

It's not the easiest travel now; the switchbacks going up the 2,225 feet of the pass from Santa Barbara test the carsick. But it used to be quite a bit tougher. This territory was home to the Chumash Indians, whose paths over the Santa Ynez Mountains created the original pass. These tribes were equally at home on the coast—some of them commuting to the Channel Islands that are visible off the western shore—as inland. Their inclination, in any case, was not to develop the land but live with it. About all they left behind were some gravesites and a grotto known as Painted Cave, where thousand-year-old drawings of startling artistry, made with the pigments from the nearby earth, tell long-forgotten tales. Certainly not a stretch of pavement.

After Chinese coolies helped build a toll road over the pass in 1869—chiseling four-inch-deep cuts into stretches of bedrock for the wagon wheels—the pass became a regular route, but something of a dreaded travail as well, with six-horse Concords braving not only the sheer drops at each side but bandits as well. If the toll keepers didn't get you, charging a dollar a horse, thieves might. In the time it took to get over the hump, it seemed everybody had a shot at you. Even with road improvements at the turn of the century, it was an eight-hour trip.

The route can still be uncertain, with winter mudslides closing it for weeks at a time. But it has become more popular than ever. Aside from the views, which open up to include

Lake Cachuma as the drive flattens along the floor, there are a few interesting stops along the way. One of them is the Cold Springs Tavern, a rustic and thoroughly authentic restaurant that is a home equally to gourmands and bikers. Another is the Cold Springs Bridge, which arches thirty-six stories over a rivulet below and lures the occasional suicide. And there's a top-end golf course that is nearly unobtrusive, its fairways sometimes going brown in the summer, blending in with the surrounding pastures.

Many more people use it as a gateway to Santa Barbara wine country, a fairly recent tourist attraction. Although vintners have long known that the climate, with its mix of morning fog and afternoon heat, is uniquely suited to a wide range of wine-quality grapes, it's only in the last decade or so that tasting facilities have gone upscale enough to invite the more sophisticated travelers. On weekends there is a nice crawl of luxury vehicles along Foxen Canyon, tracing an itinerary from Firestone Wineries to Fess Parker's to the Zaca Mesa Winery. You could spend a worse afternoon, lazing on the parklike grounds of one of these wineries, a case of Syrah in your trunk, the sun on your arms, a light buzz in your head.

Although plenty of the cars that crest the pass are heading to the wineries, many more are going to the Chumash Casino, an Indian gaming emporium of the sort that is springing up all over the country, and in the unlikeliest pockets. So far I'd had to use a little ingenuity, even imagination, to fully penetrate our gambling culture. I could travel easily to Las Vegas—and without the slightest bit of imagination—but the rest of my itinerary, mapped on the fly, had been less obvious. Dogs and CEOs, Mormons and poker, Daughters of the American Revolution and West Virginia slot halls—my premise had been that gambling was everywhere, and yet I was surprised that it was quite literally . . . everywhere. And now here it was at my back door, twenty minutes away, in Santa Barbara wine country. And how had that happened? My own neighborhood casino?

Like many in California, this particular one has evolved slowly, right under my nose, beginning its life on near-worthless reservation land as a bingo parlor, in time becoming a full-blown Las Vegas–style casino, with top-flight entertainment, extravagant buffets, a four-diamond hotel, Jaguar giveaways, and the constant jingling of two thousand slot machines.

Across the country, Native American tribes have been taking advantage of a strange loophole of both legal and taxable benefit to create an enormous gambling phenomenon. And everybody seems to be loving it. The last study, conducted in 2005, shows that Indian gambling has grown eight times faster than non-Indian casino gambling (after a decade of double-digit growth) and that, in 2004, Indians pulled in $18.5 billion—twice the take of Nevada casinos.

However the presence, or rather the success of the casino, has caused what the locals like to call tension and what the Chumash like to call racism. It may be that nobody truly enjoys a get-rich-quick story unless it's his own. Or it may be that the dominant culture of weekend ranchers simply prefers the downtrodden to remain downtrodden. Or at least not become quite so dominant as themselves. In any case, the surprisingly ascendant Chumash are finding themselves at never-ending odds with their neighbors, who once tolerated them with gift baskets but now are decidedly less charitable.

This sort of conflict is a natural byproduct of Indian success, probably any success, but I haven't seen or heard of similar ugliness anywhere else. American Indians have historically gotten the short end of the stick and have endured a mix of contempt and sympathy for as long as they've been fending off the European invasion. But now, newly rich and politically powerful, they have excited resentment, fear, and hate.

Frances Snyder, a Stanford-educated member of the tribe who serves as a spokesperson, told me the American dream is apparently fine for everybody except the Chumash. Snyder, who is loath to even visit restaurants in the area for the glares she gets, said, "It's always, why do you people need more?" The Indians have gotten too big for their britches, is what it amounts to.

Gambling has historically been an abstract notion in this country, at least in terms of community relations. Once upon a time Las Vegas was the only option when it came to slots and other table games. Atlantic City provided an East Coast alternative. The racinos, popping up here and there, began to offer regional attractions. But starting in 1988, when the federal government made it legal for Indians to operate casinos, it became what amounts to a neighborhood diversion, like the nearby cineplex. You could go to the mall; you could go to the casino. Of the 341 federally recognized tribes in the United States, 223 operate one or more casinos. The upshot: There are 411 Indian casinos in twenty-eight states, one near you.

This one is near me. Like most people, especially those who bunk in Las Vegas regularly, I used to look down my nose at Indian gaming, imagining a makeshift enterprise of dubious governance. When I finally visited the Chumash Casino, I was nearly as shocked as I always am when I top that pass coming from Santa Barbara. Although it's hunkered down in a hollow—Indians were not given the most stunning vistas for their reservations—the layout was first-rate. There was some Native American theming, especially in the hotel, where artistic homage was paid to the tribe's founding elders. But mostly the motif was sheer jackpot. The casino floor, which was surprisingly vast, was filled with blackjack tables and all the latest product when it came to slots. It had the new multi-denom machines, updated to provide the exact cacophonous experience gamblers seem to want. This, in other words, was a real casino.

What I really couldn't get over was the bustle, even on a weekday. The casino does not bus in senior citizens, Atlantic City–style, so they can while away their paltry leisure with cheap buffets, slot coupons, and other come-ons. These may not have been the heaviest hitters I'd ever seen, but this was not a coin-bucket crowd. When I asked the casino manager, David Brents, how to account for such masses in such apparent isolation, he seemed almost dismissive of the question, as if it implied an ignorance he had no time for. "This market is so underserved," he said. The Santa Barbara County market? Was he kidding? He seemed exasperated. "This market is *so* underserved."

He told me he gets eight thousand visitors a day, an increase of eight hundred a day over last year. And they're gamblers. The resort continues to provide new and better amenities—the 106-room hotel, which opened in the summer of 2004, is nicely upscale, with a spa, and the Willows fine-dining restaurant above the casino fray is also getting raves, and the showroom books bigger and bigger names (Jay Leno, Whoopi Goldberg)—but the bottom line is slots. "Las Vegas is selling rooms and night clubs," Brents said. "We're a much purer gaming play."

When I asked him what that meant, bottom-line, he was amused. Whereas Las Vegas casinos are required to put all their numbers out, Indian casinos report very little and to very few. In lieu of a quarterly report, he offered this: "Let's just say, if you were to look up the word 'successful' in the dictionary, you'd see a picture of the Chumash Casino."

The smugness, though irritating, may be deserved. There are reports that the new casino, finished in 2003 at a cost of $157 million, began paying off its $150 million bond from the get-go. Each slot was earning more than $300 a day, well above a Las Vegas casino average, and the tribe was believed to be collecting revenues of more than $200 million in 2004. This may be a modest estimate. A Sacramento tribe, one of five that signed an amended compact with the state of California (the Chumash compact, the necessary agreement between state and tribe, which spells out the kinds and amount of gambling that will be allowed, usually in return for some negotiated cut, is good until 2020), disgorged an annual payment of $33.8 million to the state, its promised 10 percent cut from the slot-machine take. That means Thunder Valley, which has just 1,906 machines, earned $338 million from its machines. Thunder Valley is believed to be the most successful in all of California, but the Chumash cannot be far behind.

In any case, there's a lot of dough coming to a tribe that numbers all of 154 (that's enrolled members, those with a quarter or more Chumash blood in them). Something about a controlled environment without competition, as the economists like to say. There is so much money that the Chumash, so long impoverished that even the youngest members of the tribe recall government handouts, simply can't spend it all. The tribe sets aside 15 percent for government, services, and benefits. This includes a new health-care center, a tribal office, and a serious commitment to further educating all Chumash, not just enrolled but everybody in the band. Besides a facility for tutoring, the tribe has in place a scholarship program that pays 75 percent of all costs—education, living, books—for any Chumash child interested in college.

The remaining 85 percent, which they basically don't know what to do with, is, in the words of Kenneth Kahn, at twenty-eight the youngest member of the tribe's business committee, distributed as a "dividend." None of the enrolled members like to talk too much about the dividend but, according to court documents released in 2006, it's nearly $40,000 a month, per member. For 2005, anyway, it was $428,969 a year. For being one-quarter Chumash.

The turnaround of the tribe, from being one of poorest groups in the country to such self-sufficiency, is one of the great stories of the twentieth century. The Chumash are not alone in leveraging that slot handle into the middle class. They may even be typical. If so, it means a preservation of a culture that was fast on its way out. The Chumash, for one example, are using their resources to reconstruct their language and publish a dictionary. "There's now time to practice the culture, to teach the dances," said Kahn. "We never had that luxury." And plans are afoot to build a museum across the road from the casino.

More important, they now have the luxury to invest in the future, as well as the past. The insane amount of money their casino is generating now is really just a stepping stone to economic independence down the line. The chairman of the committee, Vincent Armenta, told me that gaming, though guaranteed to the Indians in California as a monopoly through the life of the state compact, is a fragile destiny. California could insist on a much bigger take—Governor Schwarzenegger was trying to renegotiate a 25 percent cut to save the California budget during the last elections (about three times the corporate tax rate)—or simply allow everybody to compete. The Indians' monopoly could be written out of existence with a governor's signature. All he'd have to do is opt for a friendlier partnership—we call that a bigger percentage of the take—and agitate for non-Indian casinos in his state. How big a stretch would that be, anyway?

For cautionary tales, Indians have the example of the Tigua tribe, whose rollicking Speaking Rock Casino was all but shuttered when Texas won a federal lawsuit against them. A fifteen-hundred-slot outfit, with revenues of $60 million a year, is now nearly defunct. Gone are the $15,000 a year members received from casino profits.

With that in mind, some tribes have been diversifying to the point where their casino may someday be seen as an ancient artifact of their culture, like a cave painting or a tee-pee. The 190-member San Manuel tribe in southern California has been pulling in an estimated $100 million a year from their casino, going from poverty to zero unemployment, but has recently embarked on an ambitious empire-building plan, with stakes in restaurants, hotels, water-bottling plants, and office buildings. It partnered with some other tribes to open a Residence Inn by Marriott in Washington, DC. During the 1990s, with Indian gaming funding the expansion, Indian-owned companies grew by more than 80 percent, generating as much as $34 billion in revenues.

The Chumash are likewise desperate to establish additional lifelines. "It's a necessity," Armenta told me. He is an impressive figure. It was Armenta, a short, stocky guy who had a welding business in Los Angeles before returning home to the reservation in 1999, who traveled coast-to-coast in 2002, raising $150 million from investment bankers to build the present facility. And it's been him, along with his business committee, that has charted the tribe's future ever since. That future must include additional investments. Say, for example, the development of 745 acres just down the road, for a hotel, golf course, and a 355-home property for tribal members and others. "A project like that," said Armenta, "that just fits this area. It was perfect."

Quite a tempest ensued. Anybody could have predicted as much, given the battles over so many other, and so much smaller, issues. Organizations under such banners as Concerned Citizens, Preservation of Santa Ynez (POSY), and Preservation of Los Olivos (POLO), have opposed not just tribal expansion but everything from liquor licenses to off-site parking. These organizations contest the way the tribe wields its sovereign status to gain any economic advantage. The tribe, meanwhile, sees a hateful mix of jealousy and racism in almost every objection. Well, maybe you would, too. At a board-of-supervisors meeting, which had actually been held to protest a supervisor's racist remarks, the simmering subtext was more or less revealed when a Chumash elder lapsed into his ancient dialect and a cowboy in attendance jumped up to shout, "This is America, pal. Speak English." It was cowboys and Indians all over again, nobody agreeing whose America it is.

One interesting battle occurred over the liquor license the Chumash wanted for their upscale dining room (there is no alcohol served in the casino, nor, tribe officials say, will there ever be). The reaction was absurdly fierce. "One of the main objections to our liquor license," Armenta said, "was our proximity to Highway 154, one of the most dangerous roads around. Even though we're in the middle of wine country, with many restaurants all around us, already serving alcohol. Let me ask you how many people showed up at a hearing for the San Marcos Golf Course liquor license—one. None testified. That had a lot to do with racial issues, I'm convinced of that."

The Chumash did eventually get a liquor license for Willows, and vintners who had opposed the effort, or at least whose names were attached to Concerned Citizens circulars, readily offered to help stock the Willows wine cabinet.

Although that issue had been resolved, it has not been forgotten. Hypocrisy is the backstory to every possible conflict, from Armenta's point of view. "If we wanted to build a new hospital," Armenta said, "they'd oppose that." If Armenta seems quick to play the race card, it may have something to do with a history that predates the relocation of titans, celebrities, and wine hobbyists to his homeland. You might say, when it comes to community relations, there is some back-story.

The abuse of Indians has been something of a national pas-time, after all, conducted with the arrogance that only religion and government can get away with. In California, particularly, it was waged with a systematic vigor that very nearly wiped the state's Native American culture from the face of the earth. And it was waged from the get-go. Beginning with the earli-est colonization by the Spanish *entrada* of Alta California in the seventeenth century, there was pretty much a concerted effort, whether anybody admitted it or not, to get these guys off the land.

The agenda was, as it almost always is in the oppression of an entire people, mostly economic. The twenty-one Califor-nia missions, first organized by Franciscan padre Junipero Serra in 1769, were only nominally religious retreats. Conver-sion of the Indians, who had perfectly adequate deities of their own, might have been the grand justification for the coastal stretch of Catholicism, but the missions were really just labor camps, our first sweatshops.

The Indians not only lost their way of life—the Chumash had a nice thing going, living off the land and sea (they paddled their *tomol*s twenty or more miles into the Pacific to settle the Channel Islands), creating colorful basketry—but in too many cases their lives as well. The Spanish interlopers were actually better at spreading disease than gospel. Indians had no natural immunities to European diseases and were being decimated by smallpox and diphtheria. By the time the Mexican Republic, taking over for the Spanish, shut down the padres' operation in 1836, the missions had more or less killed a third of the original Indian population of California—a hundred thousand dead, about twenty thousand more than they'd baptized.

And affairs never really improved. Although the collapse of the mission system should have meant the restoration of Indian land, it instead accelerated the distribution of aboriginal turf. Mexico went crazy with land grants, allocating huge hunks of California to generals, whomever. Indians already displaced by the missionaries now had no land to go back to and were forced even further underground. And, thanks to an outbreak of malaria in 1833, another 20,000 Indians were gone. Mexican rule, which included slave-hunting, for good measure, reduced a once robust population of 310,000 Californian Indians by another 60,000. In seventy-seven years, thanks to the European and Mexican do-gooders, their numbers had been halved.

American rule proved no kinder. According to a history done by the California Native American Heritage Commission, Gold Rush miners extinguished another hundred thousand Indians.

Had this new government, becoming rich enough to afford sympathy, sought to redress this cultural catastrophe, it surely would not have been expensive. By this time, after all, there were no longer that many claimants. But California was reluctant to cede so much as an acre, even to this relative handful of survivors.

By the time California gave Indians the right to vote, in the early twentieth century, there were scarcely sixteen thousand of them left in California, and they were scattered, displaced, with lost lineages, religions, and traditions, not to mention property. Only sixty-five hundred of them were living on reservation land, the rest struggling on as ethnic fugitives. But even in their reduced numbers, they were still the subject of continued mismanagement, the whole point of their race now an opportunity for corruption and bureaucratic exploitation. In 1959, a partially restored Indian population of sixty-five thousand collected $600 apiece—getting 47 cents an acre, a third of what the state paid for domain lands more than a century earlier. Ka-ching!

This wasn't getting anybody back on his feet. The Chumash, clustered on reservation land in a hollow near Santa Ynez, had been dying the slow death of attrition, when they weren't dying the much faster death of European colonization and outright murder. Their numbers, a once-healthy twenty-two thousand (scattered among 150 villages on the coast, the islands, and inland) had withered to less than twenty-eight hundred by 1831. By 1901, when the Santa Ynez Band of Chumash Indians (one of dozens of Chumash tribes) was recognized by the federal government as a tribal nation, there were scarcely a hundred of them. A people that had once celebrated its own unique language, origination stories, arts, and crafts was fast disappearing. There was no longer much point in being Chumash, even for those that remained. The 1910 census counted thirty-eight of them. The 1930 census counted fourteen. Fourteen Chumash, some cave paintings in the Santa Ynez foothills, a story about a girl stranded on one of the Channel Islands (a fourth-grade reading requirement, *Island of the Blue Dolphins*), and the rock aqueducts the missionaries had forced them to construct to carry water to Santa Barbara—that was about all that remained of an entire culture.

The few survivors were second-class citizens, even in the Santa Ynez Valley, a horsey area that ought to have had more respect, or at least tolerance, for the "first people" they'd gone on to replace. The Chumash stayed on their little reservation (ninety-nine acres total), which the federal government had created in 1906. There were forty of them living there by 1974, isolated, unwanted, without much hope at all. It was subsistence living. The children of that time still remember the government trucks pulling into the reservation, everybody standing in line to get their share of the "commodities"—

white-labeled cans of beef, carrots, peanut butter. "We were the poorest of the poor," tribe business leader Kenneth Kahn told me. Kahn recalled life on Olive Lane, a "very, very run-down trailer park" that, as long as he could remember, had "issues" with running water.

There are reports that the remaining tribe was an unruly bunch, and that the alcoholism long associated with Indian reservations was not an unfair myth. There was no longer the tribal hierarchy—chieftains, shaman priests, basket-weavers—to enforce the old way of life, even if it could be remembered. If there was any Chumash pride, it would have been hard to recognize. They were, as ever, at the white man's mercy, which was hardly considerable. Kahn told me of Christmas on the reservation, where the "rez kids" received donated gifts. "I got a puzzle once, some pieces missing," he said, shrugging. "I cut out some cardboard to complete it."

Still, not every clan felt doomed to the dole. They no longer had access to the vast rolling hills of the valley, studded with oak, watered by seasonal creeks and rivers. The country had long since been colonized—by vintners now, the new holy ground being a wine country that had gone on to challenge Napa and Sonoma in taste tests—and the once worthless acreage had been carved up anew in yet even pricier plots. And then another phase of repopulation ensued. Celebrities were taking up residence in the valley, financial titans, too. Homes there were showing up in *Architectural Digest*. And the plots got still pricier.

The Chumash could not compete with them for land, or anything really, but were determined to wring some income from their little ninety-nine acres. And for many years they operated a campground, a stab at self-reliance, if little else. Powwows—reenactments that sometimes attracted three thousand people or more—were another occasional money-maker. Funds from one of those helped put in a sewer system.

There was no getting ahead, though, and Indians everywhere, not just the Chumash, remained victims of the American Dream. The 1990 U.S. Census found that 31 percent of them lived in poverty—per capita income was $4,478—and not for long at that. Life expectancy was forty-seven, compared to seventy-eight for the second, third, and fourth wave of Americans.

And then came bingo. Not to Santa Ynez, not at first. It was up to a couple of other enterprising tribes to take advantage of their sovereign-nation status—a technicality of unforeseen consequences, born in their original oppression—and experiment with gambling. This status, which has become the foundation of Indian gaming, is not the anything-goes policy most people think. It's simply a by-product of the Doctrine of Discovery, going back to 1823, when the United States decreed that Indians were without ownership rights and were, in fact, a separate nation that had to report to the U.S. government and the United States alone. This was mostly disastrous for the Indians, of course, but it did take state and other local governments out of the mix. It wasn't until the Florida Seminoles decided to experiment with high-stakes bingo in 1979 that anybody could find possible advantage in this strange relationship.

It was the Seminoles and, about the same time, the Cabazon Band in California, that thought to try their hand at the gambling business. They'd noticed that their states were introducing lotteries and figured what was good for one sovereign state was good for another. It was just bingo, the kind of thing the Catholic Church had been doing to raise money for years, but now for substantially bigger prizes. Anybody who was mindful of that first enslavement, at least along Father Serra's Camino Real in California, might have been amused by the irony of Indians shuttering the church's bingo halls in this little competition. Others, though, found it less funny.

Both Florida and California sued in federal court, start-ing with the Seminoles in 1979, trying to close the tribes down. That's where this sovereign thing came back to bite them. The courts ruled that the states really had no jurisdic-tion here—what legal scholars like to call the "you're not the boss of me" finding—and that if the state itself allowed a par-ticular form of gambling, same went for the Indians. And, furthermore—back to that sovereignty thing—it would be free of state control, not to mention taxation.

The result—more legalese—was a can of worms. Since only five states prohibited all types of gambling at this time, Indians suddenly had what you might call an opportunity for expansion. By 1988 more than one hundred tribes across the country were operating bingo halls, with total revenues put at more than $100 million. This was better than selling blan-kets by the roadside. This was, metaphorically speaking, the twentieth-century buffalo. A buffalo (extended metaphor alert!) that states could not shoot.

The federal government was motivated by a couple of centuries of guilt, not to mention those census figures that kept showing just how disadvantaged it had left the Indians. Suicide rates, double; alcoholism, six times the general popu-lation; family median income, about one-third. It was embar-rassing. Sure, show 'em a break. But the states, all of which had more immediate problems (the funding of schools, build-ing of roads) weren't so emotional. They couldn't stand the Indians participating in a windfall that was directly at their expense. The states had their lotteries, their pari-mutuel biz, sure, but now the tribes were flinging up huge bingo halls, taking down obscene payouts and paying zero taxes. The Pequots, which had barely been a tribe since a 1637 raid by Puritan-led militia virtually wiped them out, wrangled enough legal standing to patch together a tribe and open a bingo hall in Connecticut. By 1988 they were raking in $3.7 million a year (and on their way to becoming the largest casino in the world—Foxwoods Resort and Casino).

So, there was some tension. California sued the Cabazon and Morongo Bands over their card and bingo games but was essentially scolded as hypocrites by the Supreme Court. In 1987 it ruled in favor of the Indians, noting, "California itself operates a state lottery and daily encourages its citizens to participate in this state-run gambling. California also permits pari-mutuel horse-race betting." Sensing this was going to get out of hand, Congress acted in 1988, passing the Indian Gaming Regulatory Act (IGRA), settling the issue once and for all—it hoped.

The act essentially forced states to reach a partnership with tribes, to negotiate compacts with any of them that wished to move beyond bingo and into Las Vegas–style casino gambling. Well, a lot of them did. States resisting this movement could risk litigation; states embracing it might get a cut of the proceeds. What to do? One by one, it seems, the states have been made to broker a reluctant agreement with the tribe (or their managements). The Indians, savvier than they used to be (and with better lawyers), were tearing the tiniest loopholes (say, finding that a state has allowed charity Monte Carlo nights, thereby opening the door for a full-blown casino) to shreds. This wasn't necessarily the idea of IGRA, ushering in casino gaming in monopoly-type situations, especially in states that otherwise prohibited it, but it was hardly the first time that U.S.-Indian relations had produced an unintended consequence. It was the first time the Indians came out on top, though. As one case after another went the Indians' way, somebody observed, "The IGRA may fairly be said to be the first Indian victory since the Little Bighorn."

The Chumash had jumped on the bingo wagon almost as

soon as they could, opening a parlor in 1983. They still speak of the glory of the reservation's "sprung" building (which we call "tent") and the crowds they'd pull from as far away as Los Angeles, San Francisco even. The enterprise was only intermittently successful, though, foundering twice for the usual reasons—business partners (one of them Wayne Newton, who left them in 1990 with a $250,000 debt). It wasn't working quite so well for them, after all.

But a foray into slot machines proved more profitable, if quite a bit scarier. The tribe got together $600,000 and, against the express legal advice of the state of California (which other tribes had been so far successfully ignoring), installed 210 of these beauties in their "sprung" building in 1994. None of the Chumash could be certain how this would play out. The threats were real enough that the tribe had their vendors bring the games in during the wee hours of the night.

Their unease was soon offset by the cash that came pouring in. Each machine was collecting $300 a day. And that was just the start. After installing 350 more slots, according to the *Los Angeles Times*, the tribe was raking in $70 million a year by 2000, and keeping 69 percent as profit. The Chumash had performed their last powwow, stood in line for their last can of Spam, and pretty much said good-bye to Indian life as they had known it.

This was happening all across the country. Tribes that had the advantage of federal recognition, good locations, and shrewd management were creating mini–Monte Carlos throughout the land. At first these were comparatively ramshackle enterprises—a "sprung" building was a kind of starter casino for more tribes than just the Chumash—often with substandard games and weird rules. It was not a true Las Vegas experience. But it was close enough, especially in pockets of the country that had never enjoyed easy access to the real thing.

The success of these casinos on out-of-the-way reservation land has been one of the more astonishing stories in the annals of gambling. It turned out most people didn't care all that much whether Elton John would be entertaining onstage, or even if there was a decent buffet. Proximity seemed to trump glamour every time. Who needs the Strip when there's the much-closer road to Uncasville? And speaking of Uncasville: The Mohegan Sun, fifteen minutes from Foxwoods and somewhat later to the party (opening in 1996), is no longer a backwater pull-tab parlor. Second-largest property in the world, it now has sixty-three hundred slot machines on nearly seven acres of floor space, a Michael Jordan Steakhouse, a WNBA team (the Connecticut Sun plays in its ten thousand-seat arena), its own planetarium, and a thirty-four-story hotel with twelve hundred rooms. The $1 billion expansion that made room for all this shouldn't be too hard to make back: The monthly slots win for the Sun is close to $70 million. And you'd never heard of Uncasville.

No tribe has duplicated the Pequots' or Mohegans' success. Their Northeast location—they draw from 22 million people within a two-and-a-half-hour drive—will be tough to beat. But cumulatively the Indians are doing a pretty good job of recovering the frontier. Last anybody looked, there were 411 Indian casinos, run by 223 tribes in twenty-eight states. That's out of 341 federally recognized tribes. In 2005 they had gambling revenue of $22.6 billion, up from $18.5 billion the year before, and $16.7 billion in 2003. The annual take has dwarfed that of Las Vegas—doubled it, in fact. And it's going to continue to grow year by year, as tribes successfully petition for federal recognition and open even more casinos.

The Indian build-out shows no signs of slowing. Tribes that stood in line for government cheese just a decade ago are either wallowing in obscene profits or making plans for them. Every day there is news of one tribe or another, its progress toward federal recognition, land claims, a casino of its very own, or just further development of an existing gold mine. And as far as state government goes, they've been in a winking partnership; thanks to IGRA, the tribes can pursue any type of gambling they want, as long as they reach agreement with the governor in a compact, which almost always spells out revenue sharing. Only a cynic would call that payola. In any case, Indian gaming is booming. Here is just one week's worth of news briefs, from early 2006:

The Shinnecocks ran into more trouble, trying to put their eight-hundred-acre Southampton waterfront site into federal trust, when the U.S. Department of the Interior said it wasn't bound by a district-court decision that said earlier the tribe was just that, a tribe living on ancestral land. The Shinnecocks, who have been angling for recognition since 1978, were plunged back into the process, now forced to wait at least another four or five years before the Bureau of Indian Affairs can review its application. The BIA says 17 tribes are ahead of the Shinnecocks in its narrow pipeline. It says 213 other tribes have begun the application process. On average, the BIA takes fifteen years to work an application through to a decision.

The Gila River Indian Community broke ground on an $8 million expansion of its Vee Quiva Casino near Phoenix. That would bring casino floor space to eighty-nine thousand square feet. It's one of three casinos on the reservation.

The Senecas began soliciting architectural proposals for its Buffalo Creek Casino in downtown Buffalo. The Senecas, who are still fighting a group of Buffalo residents over their sovereign status, have until December 9, 2007, to open a casino under its New York gaming compact. They were planning a floor that could hold twenty-two hundred slots.

The Unalachtigo Band was demanding return of Indian land sold out from under their moccasins more than two hundred years ago so that they could build casinos with forty-five thousand slot machines. Problem: About sixty-five hundred people have since located on the site. The 108-member band said it would take a couple of fifteen-hundred-acre plots instead.

In Wisconsin, the Potawatomi tribe and the Menominees were battling over archaeological records to determine who has ancestral rights to prime casino land on the Lake Michigan waterfront. Neither has a reservation there and, since governments are increasingly critical of off-reservation gaming, must prove some connection to the land for approval. The Menominee tribe is hopeful, since its proposal of an $800 million complex right off Interstate 94 might bring in $500 million a year (though it would ding Potawatomi profits at its Milwaukee casino).

In some other news, a La Jolla band moved ahead to upgrade its thirty-machine slot arcade inside a convenience store to a five hundred-slot operation in a thirty-five-thousand-square-foot casino. The Stillaguamish in the state of Washington said it was going to grow its rural outpost by 50 percent, increasing its $30 million yearly take by as much. BIA officials rolled into Cape Cod to go over genealogy records and determine whether the Mashpee Wampanoag tribe was legit. And so on.

These news nuggets, not even a week's worth, really, bespeak the various triumphs and travails in this new culture, where formerly beleaguered nations are flexing their newly sovereign muscle. With so much at stake, there's hardly any wonder they would enter into what amounts to a generational hassle, bucking bureaucracy and, in some cases, their own lifespan. For some Indians, after all, this is twenty-first-century cathedral-building, the result so far down the line that patience is mocked. There are tribal elders who will never participate in this payoff. But that payoff is so great, so overwhelming, that nearly anything can be endured for its prospect.

That payoff is also great enough to inspire a lot of tom-foolery in its pursuit. "Reservation-shopping" is one term that springs to mind. That's where tribes basically become a front for a potential casino, investors backing the project, managing it, and reaping most of the profits. This is also a politically charged term, since it implies an all-too-convenient portability of the Indian gaming experience. Tribes who weren't lucky enough to have situated their burial mounds next to a freeway interchange—that kind of prescience would be powerful med-icine, would it not?—might be inclined to put their casino off-reservation, say, in downtown Detroit. Or, in the case of the Cowlitz, a tribe which has had no land at all, in Ridgefield, Washington. Right off Interstate 5.

The reason the Cowlitz have had no land of their own is because the Indian Claims Commission "bought" all of it—1,790,000 acres of rich timberland, for 90 cents an acre—after World War II. That's the reason they have no money, too. But with backing from the Mohegan Tribe (which has some), they've bought 150 acres and floated plans to build a 425-slot resort. Most believe that figure would grow mightily once the nearby Seattle population discovered it, perhaps creating a massive facility with nearly four thousand slot machines. For the Cowlitz, this would be as much payback as payoff, of course, but state's governors so rarely approve this kind of project that it's hard to take the phenomenon of "reservation-shopping" very seriously. Since IGRA, there have only been three instances of a tribe with an existing reservation, much less a landless one, plopping a casino in somebody else's back-yard.

Still, with so much money in play, it would be naive to think it couldn't happen. It's not unknown for entrepreneurs to invest in wannabe tribes, hoping to participate in an eventual cash flow. Donald Trump poured $9.1 million into an effort to get the Eastern Pequots recognition in Connecticut. Two other businessmen invested $20 million in the Golden Hill Paugussett there. This isn't illegal but it's at least cynical; not too many years earlier, Trump had criticized any Indian gaming that seemed a little too close to his properties in Atlantic City. He called it a fraud.

But the conflicts are huge for about everybody. State governments can listen to local opposition—who wants a casino down the street?—but cash-poor governors must also turn an ear to the clinking of coins every casino represents. Even though the state can't tax a sovereign nation, it can effectively impose a tax in whatever compact it reaches with a tribe. And, unless the state already allows casino-style gambling, there's got to be a compact. In Connecticut, where Foxwoods and the Mohegan are doing $2 billion in business, that means a 25-percent partnership, about $400 million for the state and local governments. It's so hard to be judgmental with that kind of dough rolling in.

It's just as complicated on a personal level. The question "What does it mean to be Indian?" is no longer an ideological construct. Not if the tribe is distributing millions in excess income. These days it's as much about the ability to buy Jet-Skis and vacation property as it is heritage. Just as the difference between being a federally recognized tribe and simply a historical artifact is worth millions, so is the difference between being an "enrolled" member and the chief's third cousin worth a whole new way of life. The criteria for tribe membership are different, ranging from as little as one-256th tribal blood to one-quarter, but in the case of an income-producing tribe, it can be ridiculously critical.

In Temecula, arid turf south of Los Angeles, some of the 130 disenrolled members of the Pechanga Band of Luiseño Mission Indians are battling for reinstatement, hoping to prove a history of residency or lineage. At stake is the $120,000 a year, which the 990 enrolled members receive. This is hardly an isolated example. It's been reported that fully one-fifth of California's sixty-one compact-holding tribes have membership disputes just like that.

And in Oklahoma, where the Five Civilized Tribes are reaping the benefits of the WinStar Casinos and others, so-called black Indians, or Freedmen—Cherokees born into slavery— have been lining up for DNA testing to prove their heritage. Everywhere tribes have become increasingly restrictive in their membership. The Grande Ronde tribes, who run the Spirit Mountain Casino outside of Portland, Oregon, had added 1,274 members upon the casino's opening, but have since changed their enrollment rules so that only Indians with one-sixteenth blood quantum can be part of the tribe.

You can believe that disenrolled Indians have been crying foul, charging that their brethren are only interested in culling membership, whether by blood or $200 DNA tests (government records are sometimes a joke when it comes to proving blood relationship), to fatten their own wallets. Less to share. It is a galling irony that the formerly dispossessed, a people that suffered some of the worst discrimination possible, are now denied recognition, either federal or tribal. Of course, it goes the other way, too. Folks who never wore a ponytail before are now in full war paint, hoping to claim some easy dough. Applications are up everywhere. And some Indians whose blood gives them tribal options, have been switching memberships for pay raises. There is no satisfying everyone. Indian gaming has enforced a bitter truth: Among the First Peoples, there are second-class citizens.

The Chumash have been lucky, achieving recognition and financial independence on their own. The government put their land into trust long before there was any economic reason to do so, officially recognizing the Santa Ynez Band in 1901, getting through the BIA bottleneck with about a century to spare. And the band was small enough, and concentrated enough, too, that membership disputes have never been a problem. There are just 154 enrolled members, those with one-quarter blood quantum, and most can additionally trace their roots to one of two families. It's a close-knit clan, a bunch of cousins, really.

Most important, the Chumash have avoided any corporate entanglements, becoming the rare do-it-yourself tribe. Wayne Newton wasn't invited along on this ride. Nobody was. Or maybe nobody else saw the value in a reservation that was 125 miles from Los Angeles, 300 from San Francisco—in the middle of nowhere.

There is no question that the Chumash were clueless. They didn't go into this armed with a marketing plan, a business model, a map showing concentric rings of population. They didn't hire a management team, go partners with an existing casino, or enlist Donald Trump's advice. They had the encouraging example of other tribes in California that had gone casino, but that was about it.

They have been hard pressed to really enjoy their success, though. The money has brought an unwanted scrutiny, a surprising resentment. There cannot be a story about their success without mentioning their easy money, their vacation homes in the Sierras. When district supervisor Gail Marshall was quoted in a book saying the Chumash are "not real sophisticated people who don't want to be educated" and that they "blow their gambling revenue buying new trucks" and that "when you get $300,000 a year for sitting on a couch watching a Lakers game, you're setting a role model for future generations," she was simply, if ill-advisedly, articulating a growing bitterness over the tribe's new wealth.

In fact, it's not quite like that. Of the 154 members who qualify for that money, 101 are over fifty years old. They had a long life without running water and now, if they want, they can take a cruise. As for the goodies supposedly cluttering front yards, yes, I saw some high-end trucks when I drove through the reservation. But what I was mostly surprised by was the ordinariness of the housing—manufactured, for the most part, on tiny lots. There appeared to be some neighborhood competition when it came to constructing walls and fences, but otherwise I couldn't help but think this was a neighborhood I'd move out of as soon as I got my first casino check. Instead, there is a waiting list for housing there that has more to do with family than showing off. "Why wouldn't you want to live there?" Frances Snyder asked me. "With all your cousins. It would be fun. I'd love to be able to live there."

Kenneth Kahn is the kind of guy who seems oblivious to every possible slight. While others grumble about their position in the community—second-class citizens all the way—Kahn is able to joke about their new status and poke fun at everybody's new interest in BMWs, Ferraris, and Land Rovers. It's a fact; they do have money. But not, he points out, Santa Ynez retired-on-a-vineyard money. "Let's face it," he said, "we've struck it average. We're middle class now."

Still, even that's too much for a lot of people to take. When the Chumash tried to branch out from the casino business and develop a property two miles away, the reaction was swift. At heart was a partnership with Fess Parker, the one-time *Davy Crockett* star, who has since become a player in wines and hotels. The proposal called for Parker to sell half of a giant plot of land he'd bought in 1998 to the Chumash and to develop a resort and housing. As soon as plans for the proposed resort got out in the spring of 2004, they were named public enemy No. 1 (along with Parker) by Concerned Citizens, whose concerns seem to be entirely about the Chumash.

The community—led by the valley's celebrity residents, such as David Crosby, Bo Derek, Doc Severinsen, and Bernie Taupin, Elton John's song-writing partner—proposed boycotts of Parker's existing properties, and some of them even organized a wine-dumping. Armenta and the rest of his tribe got more than just a cold shoulder; it was hardly possible for them to leave the reservation, so scathing were the remarks. Armenta called one public meeting a "lynch mob."

The advertising onslaught continued with Taupin, a British newcomer to the valley (he bought a ranch there in 1992), taking out full-page ads in the *Santa Barbara News Press*. In the most memorable of them, he promised to defend this "pastoral wonderland we cherish" and that he would "snap at Mr. Parker's lanky heels till his skin is raw." The first response to a line like that: And Elton John is the gay one? The second, which Armenta immediately supplied to the *Los Angeles Times*: "Where does a foreigner get the gall to tell the First Americans what we can do with our own land?"

Or rather, what right does anyone have to prevent the Chumash from reclaiming what was once theirs, whether by gambling proceeds or political might. But the one thing this skirmish has established for certain, even after the deal fell apart when the tribe and Parker couldn't agree on partnership details, is that the Santa Ynez Valley is zoned irony-free.

The Chumash were plainly discouraged by the opposition and became ever quicker to frame the debate in terms of race. Of course, there are reasonable objections to plopping a resort, or even a casino, on a "pastoral wonderland," and you needn't be a racist to bring them up. It is not racist to wonder if the tribe is gaining an unfair advantage, enjoying zoning regulations and tax laws much more favorable than those of their neighbors.

Like any newly franchised group, they bear watching, and this goes well beyond race. Gaming money has given many tribes the kind of political clout their benefactors used to enjoy, and it frightens some. It ought to. One watchdog has said tribes have spent $130 million on political contributions in the last six years, influencing legislation in their favor. They all have lobbyists. The tribes' power in California, in particular, will continue to grow, as the state looks to new compacts to claim some money for its budget shortfall. The state has always salivated over the $280 million in free money Connecticut gets from its two casinos; the two most recent gubernatorial elections in California have pretty much hinged on the possibility of reaching just that kind of deal. The tribes, who are becoming the go-to guys with their gambling strike, will be crucial to state politics for years to come.

The Chumash remain hidden in a hollow, literally and politically, and, for all their ambitions, do not intend to reclaim, much less develop, more than a tiny fraction of what was once all theirs. And if at some point they do manage to compromise such scenic spectacle, if they somehow do spoil that vista at the top of the San Marcos Pass, whose fault would it be, except those that spoiled theirs first?

A Bag of Money, Getting Tossed, and Coming Up Short

Here's something I more or less promised in the introduction and it more or less happened this way and is more or less legal. But just in case my understanding of the law, as it applies to nimrods holding paper bags full of hundred-dollar bills (even in the absurdly tolerant city of Las Vegas), is incomplete, I have withheld a few details and names. Anyway, the point of this story is not so much what happened, or even to whom, as what it's like to . . . hold a paper bag full of hundred-dollar bills.

First of all, unless it's something you've been conditioned to do by daily routine (you're a drug dealer, a pimp, a college football booster), you would probably find it unnerving. I know I did. When I finally found myself alone in my car with the money, I immediately called my wife. "I'm sitting here with $100,000," I told her. "I may be in over my head." She would have agreed in any event but was especially concerned when I mentioned the amount. She had seen things go wrong with lots less.

The only thing I had going for me this time was that it wasn't my money. Not all of it, anyway. Not even most of it (but, for legal purposes, some). Still, I was in possession of a sum of cash that I couldn't replace if, for example, the draft of a passing trailer rig happened to suck it out of my car, spewing it, movielike, along the Strip. I mentioned my concerns over the cell phone. "Roll up your windows," she said.

The reason I had this money—the reason one of Las Vegas's most prominent gamblers had slid it across the table at an Outback Steakhouse—was to prove the point that sports books were refusing any wagers that might be coming from sharps. His agenda was obvious enough; he wanted his previous ease of access to the sports books restored to traditional, precorporate levels. And it was his idea to recruit *Sports Illustrated*, an accomplice in several other gambling stories over

the years, into exposing this injustice or, well, the sheer
inconvenience of it all. Of course, as he patiently explained,
there was a much grander motive at work than simply his
own financial self-preservation: Money denied at the sports
book was inevitably forced onto the Internet, where the betting could not be policed as well, and certainly not taxed.
Inasmuch as the casinos' short-term fiscal cowardice might
be harming the industry in the long run—pushing traditional
action offshore—this might be important, or at least interesting enough to sidebar a bigger gambling story that *Sports
Illustrated* happened to be doing at the time. So, in a way,
the two of us were performing a public service.

Just how had never occurred to me until our gambler,
whom I had known from similar journalistic stunts, showed
up at his favorite restaurant to lay it out for me. The idea, he
explained, was to visit a couple of sports books, represent
myself as a pro, and keep betting college football until I was
tossed. Being tossed was critical to the premise. It would
prove the discrimination of dumb money over smart, which
was required of his thesis.

"So, here's what we're going to do," he said, unfolding a
piece of notebook paper with eleven bets scrawled on them.
"We're going to bet these games until we can't bet them anymore." He promised me this wouldn't be that hard to do.
Sports-book managers were in such a state of panic when it
came to line-movers like him and his runners that it might be
possible to mistake me for somebody who knew what he was
doing. He promised again: It wouldn't take long before our
business would be declined. These guys were such chickens,
he told me, I might be DQ'd the first time I bet the maximum.

"First time I bet?" I asked. "What maximum?" I must
have misunderstood. I was used to tagging along with people,

listening in, watching. That's how I roll. "Well, I can't bet," he said. "I thought that much was obvious. Anyway, here's the lines—try not to get nicked on the price—here's where to bet and here's the money." And, as I said, he slid a small bag with handles across the table. It was a little bigger than a lunch sack, but not by much. I looked inside. "That must be . . ."

"It's $100,000," he said. "You want to be careful in the parking lot with that."

I gave it a better look inside my car. It was all bundled, some in $10,000 packs, some in $5,000. Not many people see so much cash in a paper bag and are not, by the very nature of the transaction, automatic flight risks. That wasn't going to be a concern here. The real problem, the way I saw it, might be bookkeeping. That is, once I took my wife's advice and rolled the windows closed. His instructions as to size and placement of bets were specific, but I couldn't imagine myself presenting a checklist at the sports book, especially as I was representing myself as an adversary, someone who deserved to be chucked. There was no way I was going to be able to account for this much action without an accountant at my side.

But that was for Saturday, rivalry week in college football. For the moment, I could enjoy my secondhand wealth, which meant returning to my room at the MGM Grand and mounding the stacks of cash in various pyramids. Oddly, I quickly grew bored, piled the dough back into the bag, and went down to the casino, the handles of the bag looped over my arm so I couldn't easily forget it under a table. Using my own money (I'm not an idiot), I enjoyed one of those nights that large corporations are able to suffer (short-term) in the anticipation of comeuppances down the line, which you already know about. I won $11,000 at a $100 blackjack table and salted the bag with my cash (satisfying a legal loophole), entering the supplement into the books. I was pretty glad to be able to do this, piggybacking a gazillionaire's picks. I'd get a story, and a pretty good payout, too.

Well, it went down pretty much as he said, more or less. At Caesars Palace, where he had said it had gotten especially paranoid, I waited for his call. After comparing timepieces, military-style, he instructed me to bet the maximum on Kentucky, plus nineteen at exactly eight a.m. Understanding the maximum to be $2,000 (who'd ever want to bet more?), I walked up to the counter and, looking side to side as if I couldn't have been more bored with the proposition, made just such a bet.

My cell vibrated to life within seconds. My gambler was furious. "You have to bet the maximum!" he was shouting. "They'll never take you seriously. Get back there, bet $7,000, quick, same game." The most frightening thing wasn't that I was bobbling this whole scheme—I expected that would come to pass—but that he had known what and when I had bet. Was he wired into the system? Was I being watched? What else was going on behind the scenes? I bet again, looking even more bored, then walked away, per instructions, to consult my sheet and grab another stack from my bag.

And so it went. The crowd around me was fairly delirious, with a lot of Ohio State fans facing off a Michigan contingent, dozens of huge screens around us, the broadband equivalent of Dante's *Inferno*. I permitted myself a smirk of self-satisfaction, imagining myself above this partisan fray. Were they carrying gift bags with $100,000? I thought not. I was doing serious stuff here, tilting odds, flinging huge sums of cash at fate, daring it to deny my rightful and rich destiny, plunging myself into the maws of probability, joining the world of risk-takers, massaging the future to my advantage.

I was going a little nuts, basically. On my fourth, increasingly torpid trip to the counter (I waited for a call each time, becoming ever more precise in my timing and betting, and did not get yelled at again), it finally happened. A manager from behind the counter, who'd been watching this charade, appeared and, while not actually kicking me off the premises, said my day was done here. He'd pegged me for a wise guy, the type of bettor who could bring this whole operation down, probably cost him his job with my obvious inside information. My action was no longer welcome.

I couldn't have been prouder. It was no longer about proving the story; I had been recognized as somebody who worked beyond that science of incomplete knowledge, somebody who had mastered this little part of the universe, somebody who was right far more often than not. Of course I was only somebody with a piece of notebook paper and somebody else's money, but still . . .

There was nothing left to do but return to my room and watch a little football, then make my rounds, divide the winnings, and settle up. As it happened—and this should be a lesson to all you would-be wise guys out there—there wasn't that much making of rounds to do, very little dividing of winnings, and not so much settling up. To my horror, eight of "our" eleven picks were losers. This should also be a lesson to sports-book managers: Take as much of everybody's money, smart or dumb, as you can.

So, all I had to do was retrieve the paltry winnings, stuff that money back into the sack, and rendezvous with my gambler. Back at Caesars, I thrust all the betting slips forward, letting them sort the winners from losers, took the miserable remainings, and disappeared, no longer so sure of myself. That night, as per instructions, I met my gambler at the parking lot of an In-N-Out burger place way off the Strip. He pulled up in a sleek Mercedes coup. He was all decked out in formal wear, on his way to a charity function. He laughed at our luck. "Pretty pathetic," he said. And off he went.

That wasn't the last I heard from him, though. As I expected, I screwed up cashing in the betting slips, one of the games (a winner!) not quite final when I did my collecting. That's a bad phone call when a gambling titan calls you at six a.m. on Sunday and advises you he's $9,000 short and do you know anything about that. Luckily—the only luck we had among us that Saturday—I had saved all the slips for scrapbook purposes. Sure enough, among them was an uncashed winner.

I returned to Caesars, a little of my smugness called up for the occasion, got my dough, and drove off to a different In-N-Out parking lot to settle up—for good, I hoped. I was somewhat humbled by the experience, as much by my incompetence as a bet-runner as by our luck, which after all included the turnaround of most of my $11,000. My gambler, who'd lost quite a bit more, didn't seem to mind, laughing the whole experiment off. At least we proved our point, which was, basically, the casinos hated losing money even more than we did.

Before I left, though, to return to my square world where paper sacks held baloney sandwiches, I did a quick surveillance of the parking lot, wondering who else was there settling up, their bags fuller or maybe even emptier than mine had been. There were a lot of nice sports coupes parked at a fast-food joint, for a Sunday morning. I had become a bit addled from the whole experience, of course, my imagination inflamed by the temporary stewardship of so much cash. Still, it occurred to me, with a little shock: Was I likely the only guy in town carrying $100,000 to and from work? Exactly how far in over my head had I been? The sports coupes peeled in and out on a Sunday morning in Las Vegas, too early for burgers, NFL kickoffs coming up.

Twin Cities, Minneapolis

Volunteer Tax, Hypergeometric Distribution, and Bacon

I knew at some point, and at some place, I'd have to grapple with the idea of our lotteries, simply the most pervasive and apparently least objectionable form of gambling there is. As I rambled and gambled, it had begun to occur to me, become glaringly obvious, in fact, that we were no longer dealing with a sordid recreation, a guilty pleasure, but a mainstream pastime. Of course, I could see how corporate America had co-opted the unholy entertainment, decriminalizing just about every form of it to develop one of the most reliable, recession-proof revenue streams there are. Any first-time visitor to Las Vegas could recognize as much. The outlaws had been replaced by big business, who hiked the house edge just a little more, the tradeoff for increased consumer confidence.

What wasn't immediately plain to me was how state and local politics had been such a necessary, and even willing, partner in this transformation. But, really, there could have been no transformation—no racinos in West Virginia, no giant Indian casinos in Connecticut—if our government hadn't been able to come up with a definition for legal gambling (illegal gambling being the only kind there was for a couple of centuries). The definition, by the way, being anything that helps a budgetary shortfall, saves a politician the self-inflicted gunshot wound of asking for more taxes, or other-wise pays the bills.

The other forms of illegal gambling—exceptions, you might call them—had been part of a gradual acknowledgment, an acceptance. Still, as state governments maintained a regulatory stance in exchange for their cut, there remained some distance between them and gambling. But once the states, smelling easy money, cut out the middleman and went into the gambling business for themselves, it became harder and harder to find distinctions between legal and illegal gambling, or even between gambling and taxation. Once they began marketing their own lotteries, in the name of whatever benefit they could justify, all bets really were off.

Just about everybody has one of these lotteries, as unwieldy and inefficient a fund-raiser as you could possibly invent. The sheer popularity of a lottery is, on the one hand, a rebuke of common sense, an assault on our traditional value system, an amoral accelerant. For one thing, you can't win. Those mega jackpots are so statistically irrelevant they may as well be a fiction. To me, this was always a problem. For another, if you should win, against hilarious odds, you don't get your fair share. Another problem. A lottery is gambling at its worst, in other words, a system of public taxation gussied up in marketing campaigns and ridiculous catchphrases. But as I said, just about every state has one.

But where best to inquire into this triumph of social engineering, this strange apparatus of hope? This country's history is saturated with the idea of a lottery, which, when you think about it, is, on the other hand, strangely American. It's gambling, yes, but with the apparent application of democracy. The lottery is a commingling of desperation, a way to share risk and reassurance. We're in this together. And if it can be twisted into the service of public good, well, no wonder it has such an everlasting and permeating appeal. Yet, is there one place in this country that's more vulnerable to the poor odds and rich rhetoric of the lottery than another? Is there some community so devoted to the idea of pooling resources for the unlikely excitement of a Powerball drawing? A state where gambling has become giving more than any other?

Why, yes there is, and I'm in it, standing outside Tin Cup's, in St. Paul, Minnesota. There are probably more glamorous venues from which to access this phenomenon but I doubt you could understand it any better anywhere else. So, before we get into the idea of government, morals, and lightning-strike odds, let's visit the kind of place where it all almost makes sense. Where you could apply a few principles of math, a measure of anticipation, and possibly do some good. Or have a beer, anyway.

Here, outside Tin Cup's, a neighborhood tavern, there were four brown metal folding chairs, and on them were four of the palest senior citizens I'd ever seen, huddled under thick cloth coats against a March mist, each honking away on a cigarette. "Meat raffle?" I asked. One of them hacked and jerked a thumb inside. St. Paul's no-smoking laws, complicated beyond belief, had apparently struck Tin Cup's. There was a randomness to the policy that confounded and confused patrons and tavern-owners alike. Just up Rice Street, you could still puff away at Lonetti's; only a state inspector could possibly explain why. It occurred to me that even the best-intentioned legislation can produce a medical tradeoff: Inside Tin Cup's, the cancer rate was no doubt declining, while just beyond the door, a certain demographic was becoming subject to a higher incidence of walking pneumonia. "The meat raffle's here?" I asked again, since I could hardly believe there was such a thing in the first place, in this particular tavern or any other. Got another hack, a more emphatic thumb jerk than last time, and was sent in.

It was indeed here, and was still in progress, a young girl

hustling around the bar/dining room with a tray full of tickets. It took her all of two minutes to sell the full allotment of thirty, buck apiece, and my dollar draft had hardly been delivered before she was spinning the wheel again. All I can report is, things happen pretty fast in the meat-raffle business. "Twenty-one!" she called out over her little PA system. A sixtyish man, perhaps between smokes, leaped out of his seat, waving his ticket. He walked up to the white cooler next to the wheel and began pawing through the offerings—wrapped rib eyes, ground beef, a grouping of pork chops, a pair of steaks in cellophane wrapping. Most of the players I talked to at Tin Cup's had the same complaints when it came to the meat raffle. First, the smoking ban. Second, old-timers who spend a little too much time fondling the meat. "Look at the way he's poking at that," said a grandmother next to me. "Just pick one out!"

Sixtyish guy settled on the ground beef—a $22 value, like all the packaged prizes, this particular meat from Kamps Food Market—and returned to his table, accepting congrats along the way. Many huzzahs, and halfhearted attempts to grab his prize as he made his way. Once there, a round for his table, which now had a butcher-wrapped centerpiece for all to admire.

As I say, things happen fast. After this initial excitement, I had a chance to calm down, drink my beer, look around the room, and see what I might be up against. Older couples, mostly, who'd come down to Tin Cup's for a beer, for dinner, though definitely not for a cigarette. This was a neighborhood tavern, in a real neighborhood, two-story houses with aluminum siding up and down the streets. This was the kind of place where you were certain to run into someone you knew from down the block. As my eyes adjusted to the darkness, I could further see that not a few other customers had shrink-wrapped meat on their tables, or on the bar, the red beef (no chicken or fish at a meat raffle!) glistening through the plastic.

And here came the young girl again, the next drawing ready to go. I spent a buck, got No. 19 and wondered what I'd do if I happened to win a cutlet so far from home and indoor refrigeration. "You won't win," said the grandmother next to me. "Read a story in the paper. Numbers 3 and 19 never win." Although she would prove to be an astonishing trove of misinformation throughout our little evening together, she was right about No. 19. It was a loser. A sixtyish lady did win, but deliberated quite a bit at the meat locker, the selection no longer what it was, grabbing this one and that—making everybody mad—before hollering back to her husband: "You want the lunch meat or the bacon?" Lunch meat.

At Tin Cup's, this goes on for about four hours, twice a week, Thursdays and Sundays. There might be twenty drawings a night, whole sides of beef gone to a statistical slaughter, hogs quartered according to mathematical probability. And it wasn't just at Tin Cup's. Throughout the Twin Cities, there were at least fourteen bars and grills hosting meat raffles, an entire mewling herd being randomized, lotterized, carved apart by chance. An anthropologist might see here an ancient reenactment, the thrill of a primordial hunt, the risk in this case expressed not so much in terms of survival of a species, as a one-in-thirty chance to bring home the bacon. Or, as the crusty grandmother next to me explained over her own draft: "Drink beer, win meat. What's not to love?"

The point of a meat raffle, though, is not to transform grocery shopping into a gambling experience, or even flex our meat-gathering instincts, but to do good works. To take a chance on a New York steak is, the wonderful marbling aside, an actual act of charity. It's not much charity, as we'll see in a later math tutorial, but it is a form of giving. At Tin Cup's what's left after paying for the meat, the help, and the space inside the tavern, goes to St. Bernard's, a struggling K-12 school just blocks away.

In fact, all the meat raffles in the Twin Cities benefit one charity or another. It's the law. To wish for a pork loin is to help the St. Paul Winter Carnival at Joe & Stan's, or Midway Training Services at the Lucky Foxx Bar & Grill, or to help buy a fire truck at Old Clover Inn. When I went to the Cardinal, a corner bar in Minneapolis's Southside, I was able to take a chance on a rib roast from Everett's (which everybody there swore by) and thereby fund the Olympic wrestling movement.

It's true, you could enjoy unlimited slabs of beef, the collateral damage of cholesterol offset by the warm glow of charitable giving. At autopsy, the constriction of arteries was forensic evidence, not of a damaged heart but a giving one. Here, for as long as that organ pushed globs of fat through the bloodstream, which had fatally red-lined as the wheel neared his number, beat the heart of a hero. This poor, atherosclerotic victim had led a purpose-driven life.

In Minnesota.

Elsewhere, it's just betting on some meat, not likely legal and mostly beneath everyone's dignity. But this is the land of a thousand lakes, toasty cabins that sit on top of ice, the *Prairie Home Companion*, former governor Jesse Ventura, and charitable gambling. This is, in fact, the country's capital of charitable gambling.

Minnesota didn't mean to become the nation's leader in this category, home to meat raffles and whatnot, but has gotten there all the same. It was sort of accidental, actually. Minnesota has had bingo since 1945, which was no huge deal, but in the 1970s the game was unexpectedly becoming boffo, not so much for the $5 admission packages that promoters could sell, but for the pull-tabs they were allowed to peddle alongside, all in the name of charity. Pull-tabs were a fairly revolutionary phenomenon, just coming out about then, appealing to the lottery player that the states were then grooming. They are basically paper slot-machines, the three tabs that you pull back from the cardboard ticket even resembling a machine's payout windows. Sold for a buck apiece, with prizes topping out at $2,000. Though not once in my experience. It turned out that there's really only so much money a player could lose at bingo—how many cards can you play at once?—but no limit whatsoever with pull-tabs. It took no great effort to spend $200 a night, buying 'em up between games. Bingo was becoming beside the point.

There were thirty-seven states operating just like that, selling pull-tabs alongside bingo. But then Minnesota, in what some folks consider a colossal oversight, in 1981 legalized pull-tabs as a stand-alone game, permitting it to become the cardboard equivalent of video parker in bars throughout the state. There was no debate, consideration, any thought at all. It just got tacked onto a bill on the floor that session. "You could say they took off," Mary Magnuson told me. Magnuson, who represents the National Association of Fundraising Ticket Manufacturers, the people who make the pull-tabs, said the industry really got up and running by 1985, when charitable gambling in Minnesota amounted to little more than $100 million, about average in this country. By 1989, with pull-tabs having proliferated, it topped $1 billion.

This movement, whether it's circumstantial or Scandinavian, as some natives tried to persuade me, has turned Minnesota into the nation's leader in charitable gambling, with $1.4 billion in receipts a year. No other state comes close; Washington is second with less than $900 million, and a few other states do close to $600 million. But basically, when you think charitable gambling, you should think Minnesota.

And charitable gambling can mean just about anything

here. Last time Minnesota put out a number, there were 1,438 organizations licensed to conduct gambling, the nonprofits ranging from the Albert Lee Wrestling Boosters to the Zumbrota Volunteer Fire Department. In between, there were tiny outfits like the Second Harvest Northern Lakes Food Bank and the enormous Multiple Sclerosis Society, which pulled in $529,000 in 2005. Nobody goes door-to-door in Minnesota. No reason to hold a bake sale. Sell you a ticket instead.

It's so much easier this way. Who can't recognize the power of gambling in attracting dollars that otherwise resist donation? How could this have been unanticipated? Somebody who might not send off a check for St. Bernard's latest fundraiser might nevertheless be inclined to spend a few bucks in pursuit of a flank steak, or on a couple of pull-tabs. Of course! No easier money than gambling money. Beats a car wash.

This is hardly a new business model, no more for nonprofits than it ever was for the mafia. Or, for that matter, our country. Beginning in 1963, when New Hampshire went back to the lottery well to keep its low-tax reputation intact, states have been doing more or less the same thing with their own numbers rackets all along. Although no state classifies it as such, a lottery is charitable gambling as well, with bigger advertising budgets and skimpier payouts. That's all. It's the same idea: Take advantage of our inborn jackpot mentality to coax us into a volunteer tax. Genius!

Still, no other state has seized upon gambling quite like Minnesota has, to supplement its budget. And no other citizenry has been so flexible when it comes to embracing the supposed evils of gambling. Let's put it this way: In no other state could you dial up a Catholic school and ask to be put through to the gambling manager.

But I could and did. Mary Vancura, who holds that title at St. Bernard's, picked up and explained exactly what Tin Cup's meat raffle means to her school. "Everything," she said. "It keeps our doors open."

The Catholic Church, like federal and state governments, is no longer able to support its members the way it used to. And the Catholic Church, like those governments, has had to make tough, bottom-line decisions. One of them came in 2002 when the Minneapolis–St. Paul Archdiocese stopped subsidizing St. Bernard's school. At a school like St. Bernard's, where tuition is kept affordable (when it's collected at all; 87 percent of the students there receive financial aid) to service the community, this kind of pullout is usually fatal. The high school, which drew from outside the community, might survive. But the grade school, attended by kids from a hardscrabble neighborhood, wouldn't. "We were going to shut down," she told me.

St. Bernard's has always had fund-raisers, but, for any school, these tend to work according to the community's resources. Thus, the schools that need money the most, because they are serving communities who have the least, will raise the fewest dollars. In private education, the rich get richer and the poor really do get poorer. The St. Bernard silent auction was never going to make up the shortfall.

But meat raffles and pull-tabs might. St. Bernard's was able to talk three establishments into providing space for its pull-tab booth and its meat-raffle wheel. With so many organizations looking for venues, this is not always easy. It's gotten very competitive, in fact. The bar owners, who enjoy the extra business the activity brings, are nevertheless able to cut deals that are anything but charitable. If they don't charge rent, they get a percentage of the business. Still, there is so much money involved, almost any deal is acceptable. Managing three sites, St. Bernard's, a faltering school with five hundred kids, had gross receipts of more than $6 million in 2005.

And that, my friends, is why a small Catholic school has a gambling manager. Honest to God.

This kind of fund-raising was going on everywhere I looked. I could have gone to a meat raffle every night of the week and not seen half of them. I did manage a visit to the Cardinal, another tavern situated in a middle-class neighborhood of two-story, aluminum-sided homes, where the beef was also going to a good cause. In this case, it was Minnesota USA Wrestling, the state affiliate of USA Wrestling, the one that sends our grapplers to the Olympics every four years.

From the patrons' point of view, of course, the cause is irrelevant. Nobody was buying chances on Everett's cuts of meat because they believed in the advantages of Olympic participation. If this was patriotism, it was highly inadvertent. As far as I could tell, nobody was even aware of the beneficiary, which is only listed on a card by the booth, per state regulations. At the Cardinal, the point was the meat, coming as it did from Everett's up the street. In fact, in my meat-raffle travels, what stood out most was not the comparative worth of one charity over another, but the relative primacy of neighborhood butchers.

At the Cardinal, some of the mainstays were fairly rapturous when it came to Everett's. I had come across accounts where patrons were absurdly loyal to Angus Meats' pork chop on a stick at Joe & Stan's, but never saw this kind of devotion to a particular butcher. At the bar, when patrons heard I was new to meat raffles, winners were prodded forward to show me their prizes and allow me to fondle them (their prizes) if I wanted (I didn't). There were long discussions about favorite cuts. One lady, in her meat ramblings, recalled a restaurant that used to serve Everett's cuts exclusively. "Remember Bill's House of Good Food?" she asked. Everybody did. Here I recognized that Lutheran modesty Garrison Keillor's always talking about on his radio show. Not Bill's House of Great Food. Just good food.

One man thankful for that Everett's goodness, and the neighborhood's willingness to play for it, is Dan Chandler, a one-time Olympic wrestler and coach, who oversees a $3.5 million gambling empire. The Cardinal is one of five sites that

Chandler has, some meat raffles but mostly pull-tabs. And why? "Pays my salary," he told me.

That was his idea, back in 1990, when he presented the state wrestling organization with a proposal. He'd head up charitable gambling if it would pay his salary out of the proceeds. Minnesota Wrestling is a relatively small organization, compared to some other states, but from its five thousand members come a disproportionate number of top-flight wrestlers. In fact, since 1984, Minnesota has produced five medal winners, one in five of the last six Olympics. "As an entry," he pointed out, "that's second only to Russia."

But there'd be no head of Minnesota Wrestling, nobody to manage a grass-roots campaign to organize the state's youth at local tournaments or to keep pre-Olympic prospects going, if there weren't charitable gambling. "There's no other way," he told me. "Look, this is a social ill, lot of people addicted, I know that. And a lot of people think we shouldn't be doing it. But it's not like I can walk into some large corporation, hit IBM up for a donation. There are much more organized charities doing just that, and when it comes to choosing between wrestling and the American Cancer Society, some people might think there are causes more important than our sports groups."

So Chandler grinds it out on the ground-chuck circuit, spending far more time, he admits, administering the gambling operation than the wrestling. The paperwork, demanded by the state, is like doing your income taxes, except every month. And he's always racing around, delivering pull-tabs, paying help, paying taxes, rent (as much as $1,750 a month at one bar). All to fund a budget that's perhaps $200,000 a year—tiny by government funding standards but pretty much out of reach for anybody else. "I'd be a struggling stockbroker, except for this," he said. And there'd be wrestling of a lesser caliber, one guesses, except for this also.

Meat raffles may be the most elemental form of gambling

there is, what with the chance to actually assure survival (assuming your own freezer is desperately empty and going to the grocery store is out of the question). But, even so, it's not the only form, and definitely not the most popular in Minnesota. Leaving aside the state lottery for the moment, pull-tabs actually account for the lion's share of the charitable gambling, $1.3 billion. From what I could gather, a meat raffle was a sort of loss leader, an activity that worked as a fundraiser to the extent that it increased pull-tab sales. For St. Bernard's, for all the excitement over the meat raffles it holds, 93 percent of its gross receipts came from pull-tabs.

The same seemed to go for bingo, a fund-raising device so entrenched in Minnesota culture that, during my visit, a play was running in Minneapolis that heralded the golden age of church bingo there. Alas, that age is pretty much over. Only a few churches have bingo nights anymore, the state having put up so many regulatory hurdles it's just not worthwhile. Also, as in every state that enjoys tribal gaming, Minnesota's Indian casinos have killed the church game with their higher-stakes versions.

It's a shame, because bingo has been one of this country's most enduring games for about seventy-five years now, doing God's work since the Depression. It gained full flower during a sort of gambling prohibition, lotteries having long been outlawed after a wild fling across the country, when a toy salesman discovered this ancient European game in a Georgia carnival tent. The carny, having seen the game in Germany (it's actually derived from Lo Giuoco del Lotto d'Italia, which is almost exactly as it sounds—a national lottery), had trotted it out on his southern circuit, calling it beano, for the beans used to cover the squares. When Edwin Lowe saw it that night in 1929, he imagined a coast-to-coast version of the fad. He returned to New York and began selling twelve-card sets for a dollar, having changed the name of the game when a friend from one of his early focus groups stammered it out in her excitement. It was a silly little confection and Lowe seemed to anticipate its appeal. He even agreed to keep it in the public domain (probably impossible to do otherwise), charging competitors just $1 a year in royalties, only asking they call their games "bingo" as well.

The game proved to be a sort of gambling moonshine, satisfying a nation's thirst in a quasi-legal, underground way. And it almost immediately was bent to charitable causes, most notably the Catholic Church. The only problem, as a Wilkes-Barre priest complained to Lowe, was the game currently marketed was better suited for the parlor than the parish hall. The priest, who had quickly seized upon the game to augment the weekly take, had bought a bunch of Lowe's $2 sets (twenty-four cards each) but, given the size of his parish, was getting multiple winners. No fun. Lowe needed many more combinations to satisfy groups larger than the average family.

Bingo lore has it that Lowe approached an elderly professor of mathematics from Columbia University, challenging him to develop six thousand cards with nonrepeating number patterns. The professor, Carl Leffler, agreed, charging Lowe per card. Again, lore—Leffler was having so much difficulty toward the end that he had to charge $100 a card. I was unable to find any reference to Leffler that did not include the fact that, upon working out his six thousandth card, he immediately went insane. Lore? I don't think so.

By 1934 there were some ten thousand games a week, churches and other organizations using bingo to pool a community's resources during one of this country's worst eras. Maybe it would have caught on anyway, but it couldn't have hurt, rolling out in the Depression, when the only possible fiscal salvation came in the form of a bolt from the sky, or at least a full card. Lowe had one thousand workers in nine floors of New York office space, sixty-four presses going around the clock. He bragged that he was using more newsprint than the *New York Times* down the block.

All gambling amounts to, when you think about it, is a redistribution of wealth. Some games do this more efficiently than others. Bingo, besides being a popular and sedentary form of entertainment, was also a fantastic model for painless philanthropy, offsetting the 15-percent "charge" with a social setting and an 85-percent return. Who would begrudge a church or Lions Club such a paltry vig, especially when you could walk away with a nice jackpot?

As bingo grew, there were sporadic and ultimately futile attempts to quash it. In 1936, by which time bingo had caught up with mah-jongg in popularity, a few critics were making news. A New Jersey lawyer, noting that there were two hundred operators in his state netting $300,000 a week, filed suits, saying, "this demoralization of the public must stop at once." But you cannot legislate popularity, nor dictate morality, not against the wishes of so many. When a New York Catholic bishop decried the craze, charging that "the game of bingo in this diocese has ceased to be a harmless pastime," he found himself way out on a clerical limb, all alone. Here's what he was up against: In Cincinnati, during 1939, thirty-odd Catholic churches put 2.5 million players through their bingo halls (there were more than forty-two bingo nights a week that year), ringing up a profit of about $1.5 million.

Bingo remained the go-to fund-raiser for decades, but became almost exclusively identified with the Catholic Church. Protestants argued against it, hewing more to a puritanical point of view than their Roman brethren. Synagogues were pretty much split. But the communal bingo nights at the parish hall would eventually suffer more from competition than criticism. As Indian tribes began to push their sovereign nation envelope in the 1970s, offering high-stakes bingo on their reservations, some churches found they simply couldn't count on the inflow.

But bingo's bingo and, while it might not be the money-maker it used to be, you can't keep a good game down. When I was in the Twin Cities, there were still nineteen parlors hanging on (only two of them in churches), in addition to the two casinos outside the cities. At Roseville bingo, north of St. Paul, I found about 150 folks daubing away, hoping to turn their $10 package into a $99 Speedo or, improbably, the $1,000 Bonanza later in the evening. For a bingo hall, Rose-ville's a pretty lively venue, with as many as four sessions a day, each of them devoted to one of three charities. Again, the fact that fractions of each package were being set aside for the Roseville Area Youth Hockey Association was irrelevant to the daubers. They were, in fact, making it possible for some six hundred kids to get ice time, contributing perhaps $200,000 a year toward the effort. I didn't think hockey was much on their minds, though.

Did I say lively? Lively is a comparative term when it comes to bingo halls and, like any nonplaying visitor, I was dutifully depressed watching the action. This happened to be a smoking venue (although operators had to invest $400,000 for a system that changed air eight times an hour—to little avail, in my opinion) so maybe the secondhand haze added a layer of grimness. And then, once the caller began announc-ing his numbers, the place took on a deathly and disturbing calm. To be among so many people and hear absolutely noth-ing but the soft squeak of a colored dauber was just spooky. And then somebody would achieve bingo and, the point of the game being to see how many near-misses a player could possibly endure, there was a sort of mass resignation, every-body rolling their eyes in collective disgust. It didn't look fun, but a lot of people swear by it.

In Minnesota, bingo accounts for barely 5 percent of all

charitable gambling, close to $70 million. That number is going down every year, thanks to a dwindling fan base. As I've said, Indian casinos are giving bingo halls a run for their money, but another problem is that it's growing ever more difficult to make money running one. April Borash, the manager at Roseville bingo, told me that the state requires a hall to operate at a sixty-forty ratio—expenses to profit—to fulfill its mission of charity. This is tough, with the state then taking up to 70 percent of the profits and the city getting a cut up to 10 percent. There is very little left for charity.

"It's quite a little system," she told me. In giving nonprofits the gambling franchise, the state retained the ability to tax the proceeds. Obviously, 1,438 groups running enterprises that are extraordinarily vulnerable to misdeeds or just mistakes require some oversight. And that's expensive. But others see a more diabolical plot at work. Borash wondered whether the causes the nonprofits are funding aren't exactly the same causes that used to fall under government jurisdiction. "Didn't they provide playgrounds, youth programs?" she asked. According to her, it's one thing to transfer responsibility, if taxpayers prefer not to pay for playgrounds and youth programs. But that's not quite what's happening. The state, having shifted some of its duties to the nonprofits, has rather amazingly gained the ability to tax them. "They not only get out of having to do something," said Borash, "but they make a little money in the process."

I called Gary Danger, the compliance officer of the Minnesota Gambling Control Board. He broke the numbers down for me and, I have to say, I couldn't have been more taken aback if I'd been talking to a crime boss. Even Danger seemed to recognize the extortion implicit in Minnesota's tax structure, laughing at one point, when he described the money that goes to the state for "lawful purposes." But see if this strikes you funny. Of every dollar wagered, whether on a pull-tab or a pork chop, 80 cents needs to be paid back in the form of a prize. About 10 cents goes to expenses, leaving just one dime for charity. But wait! Of those 10 cents, the state claims a nickel for taxes. The nonprofit, for all the money it churns through, realizes just 5 cents, or less, on the dollar.

The upshot is, in 2005 St. Bernard's had to sell 5.6 million pull-tabs at a dollar apiece, raise another half-million dollars with raffles, paddlewheels, and bingo—a $6 million business—to get . . . $149,184 for its school budget. This is like building the world's largest couch just so you can collect a few more coins under the cushions. Meanwhile, this little nonprofit paid more than $388,000 in assorted taxes and fees. So, who makes out here?

Well, that's charitable gambling for you. Minnesota has been collecting $50 to 60 million a year in taxes in each of the last fifteen years (about 4 percent of all proceeds), while charitable contributions have been averaging only a little more, about $70 million (around 5 percent). Bake sale, anyone?

Of course, all of this pales somewhat in comparison with the granddaddy of charitable gambling, which is the state lottery. In Minnesota, the lottery does barely a third of the business that the nonprofits do, but out of the $408 million the Gopher 5 and other attractions brought in during 2005, the state kept $106 million. While the state requires nonprofits to return 80 percent in the form of winnings, it is not quite so generous when it comes to its own lottery. It gives back 60 cents on the dollar, keeping the rest for its general fund and a variety of environmental causes (including $400,000 it devoted to the Minnesota Pro/Am Bass Tour).

By now, the lottery is just so much background noise, the ambient hum of underclass yearning. Forty-one states have them, some for as long as forty years. Here to stay? I guess! Since first co-opting the numbers racket, states have increasingly relied on scratchers, Lottos, and Powerballs to chip away at deficits that, collectively, are north of $80 billion. In some states the lottery help is minimal, fractions of a percent. Minnesota has been banking on it for about one-half of a percent of its budget. But in others, lotteries fund as much as a seventh of the entire shebang. In any case, it is free money, a fun tax of moral ambiguity but economic necessity. North Carolina, righteous to the end, held out as long as it could until it could no longer stand the leakage through its porous borders. That day in 2005, when its governor signed one into law, it stanched an outflow of $81 million to mini-marts in four neighboring states. Had to do it.

The lottery has a long history in this country, going back even before New Hampshire's 1964 "Sweepstakes." It has a long history, period. You can find first mention in the Bible, where lots were drawn to settle land ownership, decide what animals to sacrifice, other issues of the day. The lottery was spiritually ideal, because, without any element of skill, the determination was obviously divine.

Although religion has gone up and down on the holiness of a crisply rolled hard-way in intervening millennia, it appears our first settlers in America harked back to those biblical passages, reviving the lottery at the first sign of a budget shortfall. In the department of the more things change, the more they remain the same, the English authorized America's first lottery in 1612 to help fund the Jamestown settlement. There is nothing like a Fantasy 5 when it comes to picking up budgetary slack. The early colonists used these subversive taxations to finance roads, bridges, and, when it came time to fight those who would dare tax them in more transparent ways, the Revolutionary War (a $10 ticket gave you a shot at $10,000—real money when a cocked hat cost less than a buck).

There were no demographic studies from that era, and it's hard to say if, as they complain now, the lottery was just another form of regressive taxation, a tea tax but different. However, these early lotteries may have been fairer than most, fairer than today's anyway. They returned as much as 85 percent to the players, only taking 15 percent for government revenue. Had there been a Mega Million back then, it would have been huge.

It was pretty big, anyway, responsible for quite a record of good and necessary works in Colonial America. Without lotteries, there would have been fewer roads, worse muskets, and not much of an Ivy League (proceeds helped build Harvard, Dartmouth, Yale, Columbia, and Brown).

By 1832 lotteries were so popular they were accounting for more than $53 million in ticket sales, fully 3 percent of the nation's income. But subsequent lotteries were less dedicated to the public good, and a religious and legal backlash began to form. The fever led to rampant privatization and inevitable corruption and was not counterbalanced by the feel-good effect of better highways and schools. By 1860 a lottery backlash had put all but three states out of the business.

There was a brief postwar boom, including formation of the Louisiana Lottery Company, a monster that anticipated issues still more than a century away. The company, which was actually a New York syndicate that had bought its way into Louisiana for the fee of $40,000 a year, introduced lobbying, intrastate marketing, multistate jackpots, and, finally, a kind of offshore gaming. They had offices in every major city in the country, selling as much as $2 million in tickets each month. Linking the states, they essentially gave our country its first Powerball. Twice-yearly prizes were as high as $600,000. But don't feel too bad for the syndicate; they had cut the payout to just 50 percent.

The syndicate fought off the country's consternation as

long as it could, even standing up to President Benjamin Harrison's complaint in 1890 that lotteries were "swindling and demoralizing agencies." The Louisiana State governor was forced to agree when he was prevented by an electorate from accepting a $1.25 million contract to continue the lottery. The Louisiana State Lottery couldn't turn its back on so much dough, though, and moved to Honduras. But even that got the kibosh, when courts used postal rules to put it out of business. By 1894 lotteries were outlawed in all states.

If there is one thing that history has taught us, though, it's that you can't really stop people from doing something they like to do. For seventy years the lottery was prohibited, but it's not like you couldn't take a chance on something. Forms of underground gambling included raffles, foreign lotteries, and that strange European game called beano.

But the folks kind of missed the gambling, their self-righteousness aside. Bingo took up some slack, sure, but there was still an American recklessness that needed to be addressed. Underground lotteries and sweepstakes popped up, the most notable of these the Irish Hospital Sweepstakes, which reached our shores in 1930. And there were other thinly disguised promotions that somehow accommodated both our devotion to long shots and our law-abiding instincts.

Mostly, though, there were outlaw lotteries, called "policy," "the numbers," or "bolita," the nomenclature depending on the clientele's ethnicity. The first of these sprung up, not so coincidentally, the year after lotteries were made illegal. The entrepreneurs behind these games observed even fewer niceties than the Louisiana Lottery gang and generally graduated into organized crime. But they offered immediacy (they were daily) and better odds (the payout was usually six hundred to one, much better than the states paid before, or since). In every large city these rackets flourished, the huddled poor banking on visions, dreams, and hunches, forking over as little as three cents at a time.

The game was even simpler than bingo. You could buy different combinations of numbers, up to twenty-five if you wanted to complicate the bet, but the most popular offering was a three-number combo—a "gig"—that would appear in the next day's newspaper, most often in the form of a horse-racing result (though sometimes they were linked to the Dow Jones closing number or, in one game, the last three numbers of that day's Federal Reserve Clearing House Report).

In the beginning, this was all fairly aboveboard, going down in cigar stores and bar rooms. The journalist Thomas Knox visited an early example of one in 1892, walking into a large room of a New York storefront to buy five gigs at three cents. There he found that the "assemblage is promiscuous and not at all select," but was attracted all the same. "A man stands as good a chance of being struck by lightning as he does of winning at this rate," he wrote. "Nevertheless the game is full of seductiveness on account of its possibilities and also on account of its cheapness." Although even three-cent gigs can add up. In the same account Knox wrote, "That a large amount of money may be lost at policy is shown by the circumstance that quite recently the cashier of an important law firm in New York City embezzled $125,000 of the money of his employers. When the defalcation was discovered and investigated it was found that this enormous sum had been spent in playing policy in a notorious shop on Broadway."

Except for the decline in the use of the word "defalcation," not much changed for another eighty years or so. The rackets became huge profit engines, attracting the attention of African-American toughs, Jewish gangsters, and then the mafia. Some accounts credit it with the emergence of a black upper class, or at least a new power base. It's accepted that

wealth created from Chicago and Harlem policy was responsible for the revival of the Negro Leagues in 1933. Writing
tickets for $35,000 a day in Harlem can cause a man to dream
a little.

Then in 1963 New Hampshire busted the ban. The state
didn't have sales or any broad-based personal taxes and had
been relying on property taxes to fund its business. Since no
politician ever gained reelection by proposing more taxes, the
state sought relief elsewhere. Of course! A lottery! New
Hampshire shrewdly navigated antigambling sentiment—even
beyond their decision to call it a sweepstakes—by announcing
all proceeds would go toward education. "Constantly increasing demands for school facilities, at a time when our people
are already carrying a cross of taxation unequaled in American
history, make it our duty to initiate programs which will
relieve this heavy burden on the people," argued the governor. So, it was for the children.

Not very much for the children, though. In doing their
"duty," New Hampshire lottery players produced exactly $24
per pupil that first year, and did nothing to alleviate their local
property taxes. Still, everybody smelled a winner here. New
York introduced a lottery in 1967, but was similarly handi-
capped by federal restrictions on marketing—no TV or newspaper advertising. New Jersey came on board in 1970 and,
like the two states before it, fell below projections, even with
profits of $30 million the first six months. The state rejiggered
the game to produce weekly drawings and a better win rate
and finally came up with a successful model for the rest of the
country.

Seeing what kind of money was available, one state after
another joined the fray. They had to. Beginning in 1981,
when President Reagan oversaw a reduction in government
services and taxes (not to mention an increase in the federal
budget deficit), states were scrambling to make up for cuts in

government aid. During the twelve years that he and President Bush were in office, seventeen states found lottery religion. Each passage was easy to justify, given the economic burdens states were now operating under. This was simply a "voluntary tax," when it was not in one's best political interests to pass the real kind. And it was for the children! As the New Hampshire governor put it, we were all just doing our duty. There's your real Reagan Revolution.

There were refinements along the way, most notably each state's development of instant games, daily-numbers games, and the big jackpot lotto games that produce the life-changing payouts (and most of the real marketing) we're always reading about. By 2005, this nation was doing close to $50 billion in sales. Hot stuff. But basically it's still little more than charitable gambling, a way to fund education or other pet causes.

Like a meat raffle, though, it funds far less than you'd think. The Minnesota lottery keeps about 20 percent of the receipts for itself, the rest going to prizes and administration. And in those states, where your lottery dollar is presumably going for education, the gambler is not making quite the difference he might believe. In fact, the whole premise is dubious.

In Ohio, where the government took in $2.16 billion in receipts in 2005, about 30 percent, or $645 million was distributed to education. Nice, but that amounts to less than 5 percent of the total education budget. Hardly the difference between learning 3 Rs and 2 Rs. Some studies have even suggested that states without lotteries are better off, increasing their education spending more than the lottery states. It's a depressing thought, that lotteries might make no difference at all, but that seems to be the kindest consensus. A 1998 report from the New York State Comptroller put it about as bluntly as possible, without actually calling for a refund. "By dedicating it to education, there is an implied promise that the lottery will increase school aid . . . This has never happened in New

York . . . Lottery money has never supplemented state aid; it doesn't today and it likely never will . . . In New York, as in many other states, lottery earnings have been earmarked for education primarily as a public relations device."

Of course, just as the schools don't get much money, neither do you. When lotteries insist they pay out $50 million a day across the land, bear in mind they're keeping that much and more. Their 50-percent payout rate is paltry even by gangland standards. A Las Vegas slot machine pays better than 90 percent, hardly the kind of investment you'd use to fund your retirement but considerably more fun than the coin flip that lotteries are. And as far as that life-changing cash-out, the strike that does all the heavy lifting for the marketing guys, forget about it. As far as you're concerned, it doesn't happen.

Do you remember when our old-time journalist Thomas Knox wandered into a numbers shop and guessed that a player had as good a chance of being struck by lightning as winning the lottery? Well, a lightning strike remains the operative, if overly optimistic metaphor. The Minnesota lottery, which, like lotteries in twenty-seven other states, is linked to the gargantuan Powerball to produce those headline-friendly $100 million-plus jackpots, gamely puts forth in its online FAQ that giant prizes are, in fact, more common than a bolt out of the blue. It said that in 1996 there had been 1,136 winners of at least $1 million in this country, while only ninety-one people had been killed by lightning that same year.

But that's not the same as being struck by lightning, is it? And those chances, compared to winning a Powerball or Mega Millions (which links ten states), are actually quite good, about 1 in 700,000. To compute the odds of winning the Powerball, you need to know a little something about hypergeometric distribution. And on the off chance you don't, here's the summary as it applies to the probability of winning one of those multistate bonanzas: None. The longer version: It's one chance in 146,107,962. As the guy in *Dumb and Dumber* said when informed of his one-in-a-million odds of hooking up with Lauren Holly: "So you're saying I've got a chance!"

There was a marketing slogan in California for a while, something like, "You can't win if you don't play." Well, in spite of the news some lucky group of meatpackers produces when it comes forth to claim its $365 million ticket, you actually have the same chance of winning whether you play or not. Mathematically, a 1-in-146 million chance is so statistically insignificant as to make the prize pointless. Let me put it another way: In the time it would take you, statistically speaking, to win the Powerball, you would be struck by lightning 253 times. Is that really something you want to go through?

It's cruel to say that lotteries are for people who can't add, when what we mean to say is that they're for people who can't divide. Nobody knows for sure whether the lottery appeals only to the math-challenged, but they've got to be part of that target group. And this goes to the age-old complaint against lotteries—that they are played by the least sophisticated people, those who can least afford to turn a dollar into 50 cents. Common sense tells you that lotteries have to be a regressive tax (first of all, they're most definitely a tax, in that they take in more money than they return), taking most of the money from those that don't have it. When the linked lotteries began rolling over to $300 million jackpots, it's true, the affluent begin to take fliers at the corner 7-Eleven. Who couldn't use $300 million? At those times, the lottery almost becomes a progressive tax. But mostly the players are disproportionately low-income, minorities, those with less than a college education.

If common sense doesn't tell you this, just about every study done on lottery demographics will. These studies prove the old argument, first voiced by political economist Sir William Petty in the seventeenth century, that "A lottery is properly a tax upon unfortunate, self-conceited fools." He advised that "the Sovereign should have guard of these fools, even as in the case of lunatics and idiots." Others since have argued that lotteries are just a way of recapturing the states' welfare dollars. Well, it's probably not that bad but it's not good, either. How about this: The 20 percent of players who buy 80 percent of the tickets are decidedly and disproportionately low-income by any measure. In Texas, where they do $3.5 billion in sales, a study shows that lottery players pretty much mirror the population in terms of gender, race, and income when it comes to total tickets. But when you look at per-month spending per group, it gets kind of discouraging. In its 2005 study, Texas found that high-school dropouts spent an average of $173 a month. Those with college degrees, $48. Because they know hypergeometric distribution?

For all the talk of gambling addiction, the biggest junkies are not the folks dutifully trooping in to the liquor store for their Midday Show Me, but the states themselves. This money, no matter how inefficiently or cynically it's gained, must now be maintained at all costs. There is no turning back, no raising taxes to replace it, no new bond issues to be passed in its stead. And although the idea of a revenue fairy remains an attractive one, it's still one that has to be executed aggressively to work on this large a scale. That is to say, it's not a slam dunk.

In Ohio, and other states, revenues went down for several years. But even to maintain the status quo, as most states do, they must be increasingly inventive, with new and more attractive offerings, better payouts, more drawings. South Carolina hooked up with NASCAR to sell themed tickets. The NBA, NHL, and some golfers have also sold licenses to lotteries. New York has been selling Mother's Day tickets for several years now (what better wish than "Win Up to $300,000").

More crucial: Beginning in 1989, when South Dakota first approved them, states have been going to video lottery terminals, which happen to resemble slot machines (Massachusetts was toying with a VLT machine that showed a virtual horse race). The folks like those.

And, of course, more marketing. Probably only our friend Thomas Knox can remember the day when governments were so squeamish about their takeover of the numbers rackets that they more or less ran their lotteries in secrecy. But by 1975, when the federal ban on advertising was lifted, lottery commissions have become the real easy money for Madison Avenue. The states spend nearly $500 million a year (the California account alone, which had been up for grabs, was for $125 million; Minnesota's was more modest at $7 million) on advertising and promotion. These ads almost always try to tap into our fantasy life, featuring tropical islands and mai-tais and other examples of nonspecific wistfulness.

One might detect a whiff of desperation as public finance continues to morph into the kind of oddball schemes that used to make for easy prosecution. These are tough times, but then aren't they always when it comes to funding institutions like schools. Raising money is never easy. And can it be much longer before lotteries are pegged for what they really are— another way to raise money? Or can the cheap thrill of a newly scratched Pick 6 forever cloak a subversive tax?

The lotteries might go on forever. They probably have to. But in Minnesota, there are signs that the more transparent form of it, charitable gambling, is running its course. There are hints that the concept has been flogged, if not to death, then to exhaustion. After peaking in 2000, when Minnesotans gambled $1.5 billion, there has been a slight but steady drop in activity, year by year. In 2005, gross receipts dipped 3.1

percent, dropping below $1.4 billion for the first time since 1997. Not time to panic, but perhaps time to consider some options.

Everybody I spoke with agreed: The idea had matured, used up its novelty, been plundered, picked over, and exploited beyond possible rejuvenation. The taxes were too onerous, the Indian gaming competition too fierce, the customer base either dead or tapped out. Mary Vancura at St. Bernard's said her school was used to getting as much as $300,000 out of its gambling but now, with receipts the lowest in fifteen years, was expecting no more than $100,000 a year. As educational expenses were not experiencing a likewise decline, there was understandable concern among the school board. "You got any ideas?" she asked me.

She believed that gambling money was more like an oil reserve than a renewable resource and that Minnesota had finally gone dry. She believed the initial excitement over charitable gambling—a kind of gusher that had every nonprofit roughneck throwing his hat in the air—has now subsided, now that the money has been depleted year after year. There was just so much gambling money available and, after fifteen years or so, it's simply been gambled. Gone. "The people that gambled in the beginning," she speculated, "they've lost it all."

Everybody I talked to, whether at bingo parlors or meat raffles, was working harder—more bars, more nights—to produce a little less. The magic of gambling still worked. You could still turn a package of bratwursts into a teacher's salary, but the spell was getting harder to produce and wasn't lasting as long.

Then, too, there was the matter of smoking. Nobody could have anticipated that a clean-air act would have struck a blow at both lung cancer and Olympic Greco-wrestling, but there you have it. Dan Chandler said his gambling proceeds for Minnesota Wrestling had been cut nearly in half due to nonsmoking laws. In fact, Minnesota's rather uneven smoking laws (until 2006, when most bars and restaurants became smoke-free, prohibition was based on such things as food sales and liquor sales—too complicated to discuss) have nearly crippled some nonprofits. Once the ban was even partially enacted in Hennepin County, home to the Twin Cities, charitable gambling declined 29 percent in just two months. Some bars have gone smoke-free while others, as cloudy with carcinogens as ever, poached their meat-raffle-ticket-buying customers. With an even playing field, balance may be restored in the world of pull-tabs but, let's face it, some of those smokers just aren't going to be coming back.

The kind of person who smokes, enjoys a drink, and is interested in gambling for a package of red meat may not be long for this world but is, nevertheless, pretty much the perfect profile of Minnesota's charitable gambler. At St. Bernard's they are lamenting his disappearance, even as he was likely to enjoy greater health. "I'm all for nonsmoking," said Mary Vancura, laughing, "but I'm a little conflicted about it when it comes to charitable gambling."

The other issue that might doom charitable gambling, and is much easier to foresee, is that other kind of gambling—legalized. It's just killing Minnesota that it can't get at the Indian gaming revenues, so the only thing it can do is go heads-up with the eighteen casinos already there. Talks are on the table to put a casino in the Mall of America, to put slot machines at racetracks, VLTs in bars. When Louisiana, which had a $200 million charitable gaming industry at one time, first allowed video poker, charitable receipts plunged 63 percent in the first year.

At Tin Cup's, I thought I could recognize the end of an era. The grandmother next to me at the bar was speaking for a lot of people when she said the no-smoking laws had taken the wind out of her sails, if not her actual lungs yet. "Look at me," she said, "a smoker all my life and never been sick." I did look at her and, while offering no judgment that would otherwise discourage her, wasn't ready to predict a record-breaking lifespan, either. "What do doctors know anyway? Smokers living to 104, you see them on the *Today* show." I wasn't ready to agree with this, but let it pass. "I don't even know why I come here anymore."

But it wasn't just the smoking laws. Charitable gambling is the most local, the most personal form of gambling there is. Whether it's bingo or a meat raffle, it's an expression of community, an excuse to gather, the chance to convert a wild hair into an act of neighborliness. A dollar spent on the chance to win a prime rib is not a dollar that entirely (although mostly) vanishes into a jurisdictional ether. At least a nickel of it ends up buying your nephew ice time, or helping to build a baseball diamond down the street. You are voting your dollar directly to its rightful destination, rather than taking a chance that Minnesota, once it has its slot machines everywhere in place of pull-tabs, will know what to do with it (Pro/Am Bass Fishing?). Plus, you might run into somebody you know.

It seemed to me that these connections were breaking down, though, as our lives became more complicated, more distant. These days there are less likely to be neighborhood taverns or bingo halls, the communal watering holes that refreshed our social thirst. Now we go to Applebee's, watch TV (and smoke) in our suburban living room. We don't really have neighbors (when are we home to meet them?), and are less inclined to do something for them, even if there's a chance our altruism lands us a pot roast. We're busy, we're isolated, we're a little more self-centered than we used to be. If there are problems out there—multiple sclerosis or ice time that's just too expensive—let's let our state officials deal with them, fund them however they can. As for those rib eyes, if we really want them, I suppose, we'll just buy them.

Proletarian Accuracy,
Opinion Aggregation, and Avian Flu

There is nothing like simple vocabulary when it comes to legitimizing suspect behavior. A sports book, that's just wrong. Mostly illegal, always dubious, hardly ever approved. Whatever goes on in a sports book is, at least according to most of society these days, pretty irresponsible activity. But a decision market! Now we're talking! Betting on when Saddam Hussein will be captured, well, that's not really betting, is it? That's civic participation.

More and more, you can participate in . . . more and more. Mostly it's in play-money accounts, although Dublin-based InTrade offers the ability to risk real money. And what you'd be risking it on is, in addition to the usual sports propositions, everything from the selection of the new pope to when the avian flu will first hit the United States. The variety of contracts you can buy is astounding. If there is something that warrants an opinion—the box office opening of the new *Batman* movie, a hurricane landfall—then there is a place to put your money, play or otherwise, where your mouth is.

These trade exchanges—idea futures, predictive markets—have been around for a while. It's much closer to options trading than a casino, although the middle ground suggests those two really are just points on a continuum—you invest, I gamble. In a trade exchange, you simply buy contracts on an event, your price being the probability of its occurrence. Thus begins an online argument. The price gets hammered into a number by opposing viewpoints, moving on information, sentiment, and experience. The price on New England winning the Super Bowl, for example, rises as it moves through the playoffs. A contract offered at 10 cents in the preseason might grow to 60 cents by the AFC Championships. Or dip back to 30 cents if Tom Brady breaks a leg. In any case, you'd get $1 back if the Pats do win, nothing if they don't.

There are two interesting things about these kinds of exchanges. First, as I've mentioned, there's the chance to back a belief in the interest of your choice. Previously you had to be a sports fan to find a reason to make a meaningful wager. But with everything from Hollywood Stock Exchange to the Iowa Electronic Markets, and now InTrade and HedgeStreet blooming online, it's possible to bet—I say bet, because that's really what we're talking about—on Oscar winners, Supreme Court nominees, or the median home price in your city. As I write this, I could go to the Foresight Exchange and take sides (not for money, though, that's still illegal) on whether Hillary Clinton will be elected president, whether extraterrestrial life will be discovered by 2050, or even if I'll live to see a one-meter rise in sea level (while I'm betting on when the sea will flood local beaches, my insurance company is already betting if I'll live long enough to see it; the contract on me living to see whether extraterrestrial life will be discovered by 2050, for that matter, would probably start at one cent—another story). There are people out there who would find these outcomes more important than New England's continued dominance in the NFL.

But what's really interesting about these exchanges, which are just an aggregator of public opinion when you think about it, is how predictive they actually are. Something like this happens in sports betting when the line gets moved to that fifty-fifty divider of opinion, when everybody finally reaches the betting equilibrium, paralyzed by indecision; if USC is only a three-point favorite against Texas, you shouldn't be surprised if it's a close game. The people have spoken. Or, a better example: When players make a horse a two-to-one favorite, that really does reflect its chances. That horse will probably win half its races against this field, on this day, on this track.

When it comes to the capture of Saddam Hussein, though, all bets should be off. There just isn't the information out there to make a plausible prediction. Yet two days before he was discovered in his hidey-hole, the InTrade contract on his capture moved sharply higher, for no reason that anybody could think of. Odd. But that's the way all these exchanges play out. The Iowa Electronic Market, which "sells" contracts on presidential hopefuls, almost always does better than pundits or polls when it comes to the election. The Hollywood Stock Exchange is the go-to place for Oscar picks. In 2005 HSX hit eight of eight in the major categories and thirty-three out of forty altogether.

This kind of proletarian accuracy continues to be a surprise, even in a country that was founded on democratic principles and supposedly has so much respect for the common man. The truth is, authority in any given field is especially prized and experts have inordinate sway over our affairs, and the common man isn't given the time of day, much less credit for his opinion. Maybe it's our devotion to continued education, but anybody with specific knowledge is granted elite status here.

What these exchanges seem to say is expertise is not only overrated but actually might be flawed. The experts have entrenched viewpoints, are less vulnerable to dissent, and have little ongoing error correction. The level of specialization required for expert status turns out to be self-limiting. In his book, *The Wisdom of Crowds*, James Surowiecki speculates that the "best collective decisions are the product of disagreement and contest, not consensus or compromise." The arrogance of knowledge does not brook protest or permit disagreement.

A group, though, tends to cancel out error and bias, while collecting unbelievable amounts of information, all the while averaging its conclusions. Surowiecki uses the example of the *Challenger* explosion, where the public immediately and emphatically—and quite mysteriously—singled out the cause of the rocket's failure. There were four contractors involved in the launch and, naturally, all of them took an initial hit in the stock market, the original trade exchange. Yet if you wanted to bet on the culprit, you only had to notice that Morton Thiokol dropped 12 percent, compared to the 3 percent the other three had slipped that same day. Six months later, the presidential commission found that Thiokol's O-rings were to blame.

People, turns out, think collectively much better than they do individually. It may be nothing more than eliminating the expert from the process, somebody who may end up perpetuating a bias or misunderstanding, somebody who has too much influence for his own good, in any case. Or it may be just the sheer accumulation of data, the disparate and disjointed facts that everybody brings to a problem, the nonsense out there that somehow gets averaged into a solution.

This notion ought to be reassuring to anybody whose fate falls before a jury, an assembly of sad sacks if ever there was one. As a group, they certainly make better decisions than they could individually. It also ought to be intriguing to policy makers, whose decisions are crippled by self-interest. The Pentagon, of all departments, tried to use a decision market to predict terrorist attacks. The idea was that a for-profit market would be the most efficient way to elicit information. Maybe. But betting on terrorism seemed too unseemly after 9/11, and the project was abandoned.

But how about business managers, where unseemliness is never a factor, and whose far-reaching decisions are necessarily grounded in the worst kind of ignorance? What will still be fashionable six months from now, when our designs finally hit the market? What price point will be palatable, when production does ramp-up? Who should we market this to?

Some companies have decided not to decide, or at least not everything. For several years, Hewlett-Packard toyed with predictive markets and set up a mini-exchange, allowing some managers to bet on monthly computer sales, buying and selling futures contracts, priced at $50 per. The result? The exchange players beat the "official" forecasts three-quarters of the time. Google is fooling around with the idea, too, as is Intel and many others. It's easy to see that betting on results, rather than just wishing for them, can produce a far more unvarnished truth than the usual corporate pipe dream.

The decision market may be effective for just that reason, a total lack of sentiment. A political poll can't help but measure who the respondent hopes will win, while a decision market, where there's money on the line, strips all sentiment away. You can plan to vote for John Kerry but it's hardly un-American to profit on a George Bush contract at the same time. Actually, that's the most American thing you could do.

As this idea grows, the idea that the accumulation of opinion somehow sucks the truth out of any decision, there are going to be markets for every conceivable area of inquiry. Who'll be the new prime minister of Britain? What's the next new cuisine? Which nuclear power reactor will fail first? Some will be useful, others not. But if the power of prediction really does belong to the masses, it won't be long before every important decision we face is properly framed and displayed—on a tote board, we predict.

Anywhere, USA

Hot Chicks, an Internet Clubhouse, a Cyber Stalemate

His voice originated somewhere in Costa Rica, hooked into a corporate computer in San Jose, streamed north on a VOIP line to Bodog-owned offices in Vancouver, and then was bounced south to California on a landline. As if even his conversation defied easy jurisdiction. In fact, there are few creatures so vaporous, so hard to pin down as Calvin Ayre, billionaire owner of the online casino Bodog.com and recent *Forbes* cover boy. Which is probably just as it should be in an industry that exists, for all practical purposes, in a legal and commercial ether, neither here nor there, neither real enough to accommodate physical inspection nor quite spectral enough to invite faith. Except for Ayre's actual voice, and a catalog of stagy PR photos on his Web site, it might be possible to dismiss him as just another Internet phantom, a ghostly assemblage of bits and bytes, a cosmic screensaver behind our cyber felt table.

But if Ayre was calling from anywhere, it was really the future, a time not so distant when technology will have completely transformed an elemental urge to take a risk into a thoroughly acceptable pastime, the availability of gambling so total that it will be as free as the air we breathe, just a matter of grabbing onto a few electrons here and there with the device of our convenience. When formerly policed activities become so personal that it is impossible to monitor them, much less control them, there can be no boundary to behavior. It will be an interesting frontier to finally observe, when we can bet as much or as often as we wish, without the historical brakes of community oversight. What will this country look like then?

Well, look around, because if Calvin Ayre was calling me from the future, it didn't sound like long distance. We're close. We're just about there.

Not quite, of course. Ayre's strange electronic limbo remains a condition of U.S. law and dated statutes that were erected years ago with something entirely different in mind but which nevertheless have all of us—not just Ayre—in a somewhat uncertain place. But if this is gambling's purgatory, not quite real but certainly not fantasy, it is going to be a brief one. The Internet is only the initial technology to push gambling beyond all obvious constraint; others will elevate it even further past sanction, until it will take barely more than the thought itself to exercise risk.

Here's how it stands now: An online casino—and there are now twenty-three hundred of them, beeping and pulsing out there—is obliged to operate beyond the reach of any normal authority, making each screen-shot a virtual crime scene. It's an outlaw enterprise, as far as many countries are concerned, and would be subject to the same reprisals any bookie might face, if only it was substantial enough to somehow engage, to wrestle into court, or even look at. But try as it might, U.S. law can do little more than shake its fist, mounting semi-comic campaigns to discredit or criminalize or cripple the industry, and just generally harrumph. It might just as well go after the wind.

Ayre is just one of those Internet fugitives, long gone into that wind, having set up shop in Costa Rica where he can drain U.S. dollars through a tangle of broadband plumbing, none of which ever returns. And, for a guy supposedly on the run, he sounded pretty pleased with himself when I spoke with him.

Ayre, son of a Canadian pig farmer, who has transformed himself into the new millennium Hef ("I'm having more fun than he ever had," he snorted), is not much troubled by the purgatory forced upon him. He is a happy exile. When I asked him about his fugitive status, a legal condition that the U.S. government had begun to enforce in the summer of 2006 with some high-profile arrests, he was heartily dismissive. For someone who seemed—to me, anyway—to have been effectively expatriated, the loneliness of the long-distance bookie was, even against the evidence of his PR material, surely a trial.

"Too many hot chicks here to get lonely," he said, his voice crackling over the complicated connection. "Let me tell you, five hot chicks will definitely distract a guy from his loneliness." In a fuddy-duddy, Dr. Phil way, I wondered if a guy who had just turned forty-five didn't want more from life than that. The line went quiet for a while—a moment of introspection at the other end?—before he could muster a reply. "More?" he asked. "More than five?" His scratchy laughter wound through miles of cable, boomed around in satellite space, and then reached my ordinary one-woman-to-a-man RJ-11 wire. Five hot chicks should almost always be adequate to a man's requirements, or publicity anyway.

Ayre is riding the crest of the online gaming boom, his business doubling every year for the last four, pocketing so much money that, yes, five hot chicks are not only possible but an obligatory retinue. He lives in a ten-thousand-square-foot enclave in Costa Rica, worth $3.5 million, surrounded by servants, hot wheels, and, to judge from his more or less constant PR campaign, even hotter chicks. There are lots more just like him (*Forbes*'s billionaire list has newly anointed three of his peers), but nobody so in-your-face as Ayre. It's as if everybody else is ashamed of such easy wealth, or just afraid to invite any attention. Ayre wasn't *Forbes*'s first choice for the cover, as far as that goes; the mysterious Ruth Parasol, described as the wealthiest working woman in the world when her PartyGaming went public, declined the honor. And these are almost certainly not the only online billionaires, either. The PartyGaming bunch, which accounted for all the entries besides Ayre on the *Forbes* list, was there because they had to disclose their dough in the public offering. You can bet other owners prefer the anonymity of their industry; who knows what's in their wallets?

So it's sort of left to Ayre to put a face, a very happy face, on this new business. We do know that online casino revenues reached $15 billion in 2006, with some analysts predicting another doubling by 2010. The popularity of poker has accounted for a lot of the growth, as players either unwilling or unable to access real card rooms have been attracted to online games. The sites have proliferated to take advantage of the phenomena, adding sports betting, online casinos, bingo even. It appears that consumers have overcome whatever discomfort they might have felt, sending money off to ethereal card rooms or sports books, waiting for invisible wheels to turn or make-believe flops to develop. Convenience apparently offsets suspicion. In any case, gamblers were expected to bet $4.7 billion on sports and another $4 billion in poker in 2006 in this new, unseen world.

It's almost impossible, though, to tell how well many of these outfits are doing, except in the case of online poker giant PartyGaming, which raised $8.48 billion on the London Stock Exchange in 2005. PartyGaming (making billionaires of Parasol, her husband, and the Indian Institute of Technology grad who wrote the first poker programs), with